# How to
# Establish
# an Alternative
# School

CORWIN
PRESS

**The Corwin Press logo**—a raven striding across an open book—represents the happy union of courage and learning. We are a professional-level publisher of books and journals for K-12 educators, and we are committed to creating and providing resources that embody these qualities. Corwin's motto is "Success for All Learners."

# How to
# Establish
# an Alternative
# School

## John Kellmayer

**CORWIN PRESS, INC.**
A Sage Publications Company
Thousand Oaks, California

*For information address*:

Corwin Press, Inc.
A Sage Publications Company
2455 Teller Road
Thousand Oaks, California 91320

SAGE Publications Ltd.
6 Bonhill Street
London EC2A 4PU
United Kingdom

SAGE Publications India Pvt. Ltd.
M-32 Market
Greater Kailash I
New Delhi 110 048 India

Printed in the United States of America

**Library of Congress Cataloging-in-Publication Data**

Kellmayer, John.
    How to establish an alternative school / John Kellmayer.
        p.    cm.
    Includes bibliographical references and index.
    ISBN 0-8039-6257-6 (cloth: alk. paper).—ISBN 0-8039-6258-4
(paper: alk. paper)
    1. Free schools—United States.  2. Problem children—Education—
United States.  3. School management and organization—United
States.  I. Title.
LB1029.F7K45  1995
371'.04—dc20                                                    95-19343

This book is printed on acid-free paper.

95  96  97  98  99  10  9  8  7  6  5  4  3  2  1

Sage Production Editor: Astrid Virding
Sage Typesetter: Andrea D. Swanson

# Contents

# Preface

## How to Establish an Alternative School

*How to Establish an Alternative School* is dedicated to approximately one thousand "difficult" young people who for more than 20 years I've had the pleasure to work with as a principal or assistant principal at one of three public schools. One of these schools was a countywide alternative high school for chronically disruptive and disaffected teenagers. The second school was a countywide program for emotionally disturbed teenagers. The third program was situated at a traditional high school, where I was responsible for an after school program for students who were considered to be hard-core discipline cases.

As administrator of these three schools, I dealt on a daily basis with a wide variety of emotional and social problems, including dysfunctional families, sexually transmitted diseases, teen pregnancies, violent outbursts, substance abuse, runaways, weapons offenses, gang involvement, depression and suicide, eating disorders, and juvenile crime. Some of these young people had tragic histories—girls who had been raped or who were victims of incest; another girl who had witnessed her mother's suicide; a boy who while drinking had accidentally burned down his parent's house, killing his little brother and sister.

The memories—good and bad—of these young people will remain with me forever. I remember one bitterly cold Monday morning, with the wind biting the ground like teeth, when I walked from classroom to classroom to tell students that one of their classmates had committed suicide over the weekend. I remember the hundreds of teary-eyed faces as I delivered a eulogy at the viewing of a 17-year-old girl who had been killed in a traffic accident. Then there were the fights that I broke up; the time my car was shot at; the weapons that I confiscated from students; incidents in which I was spit on and punched; times when I discovered students had been drinking or using drugs; situations when I cleaned up vomit from drinking and blood from fights; and the countless number of times that I was cursed at or threatened.

Despite the best efforts of myself and their teachers, it often seemed that nothing worked with most of these teenagers. Many teachers "burned out" and resigned their positions. One who resigned said that, "It was like teaching in a zoo." Those who left often blamed me for not getting "tough" with the students. One ex-teacher told me, "It's your job to break their spirits and prove once and for all who's boss."

Although enormously frustrated with the behavior of these adolescents, I was convinced that their negative behavior was symptomatic of deeper psychological and emotional problems. I was further convinced of the futility of simplistic "get tough" approaches such as TOUGH LOVE and Scared Straight. Just as a physician wouldn't think of scolding an influenza patient for coughing or shivering when the patient entered the doctor's office to seek treatment, I believed that it would be unconscionable to become angry with students who had a history of hostile behavior for behaving in a hostile manner when they entered these schools. There's no on/off switch to psychological and emotional development. It takes a long time to heal a damaged child. The passage to self-awareness involves a life-long journey for each of us—child, teenager, and adult. That journey is particularly difficult for adolescents.

These troubled young people needed *comprehensive programs* to address their problems—not simplistic, get-tough solutions.

As their teachers and I weathered storm after storm of problem behavior—as we were tested every day with curses, threats, and worse—almost miraculously one after another of these young people slowly began to change, to heal. For as time passed, as I got to know them and they came to know and trust me and their teachers, their behavior improved remarkably. It was as if a window had been opened to their minds and souls. And when that window had finally opened, they were ready to learn. The great majority went on to earn their high school diplomas and to experience success in college, the military, trade school, or in the workforce. Many have come back years later to thank me and their teachers, saying if it wasn't for the help that they received in these alternative programs, they never would have made it. More than a few have told me that if it wasn't for that help, they wouldn't be alive today.

Despite the negative incidents (and one doesn't spend a career working with at-risk teenagers without accumulating a whole lot of negative incidents), *without exception* I hold positive memories about every student who ever insulted, harmed, or attempted to harm me, as well as the many other students—teens who never harmed anyone but themselves—who attended these alternative schools. I don't mean to give the impression that the majority of these young people were hostile. In fact, most of the hostility was directed inward in the form of self-destructive behavior. Psychologists explain that young people respond to unpleasant situations in one of three ways: fight, flight, or surrender. Though we had our share of fighters at these schools, more common were students who fled or surrendered. Often their flight took them down the road to depression, under-achievement, substance abuse, or promiscuity. Fugitives from their own futures, these were intelligent teenagers who—overcome by a sense of powerlessness—had simply stopped trying.

Regardless of their behavior, all of these young people shared something in common—they had been hurt and were confused. In response to that pain and confusion, they tried to hurt others or themselves. This book is dedicated to those one thousand teenagers. It is also hoped that readers of *How to Establish an Alternative School* will use the ideas presented here to start their own programs and to redirect the lives of at-risk youth throughout the United States.

## The Genesis of This Book

I decided to write this book for three reasons. First, for several years I have been consulted by many districts or consortiums of districts, or have been asked to give presentations by various depart-ments of educations, universities, and so forth on the topic, *How to Establish an Alternative School*. I felt that I could have a greater impact on helping to solve the problems of at-risk youth by writing down my ideas and suggestions in a comprehensive manner. Second, as the need for programs for at-risk youth has become much greater, I have become increasingly distressed at the number of punitive, ineffective programs that are masquerading as "alternative" schools. Finally, I had the opportunity to serve as a moderator of a panel discussion on disruptive students at a national conference of school administrators that was held in Fort Lauderdale, Florida. The panel that I moderated presented and examined various perspectives on discipline and disruptive students, with an emphasis on applying what the most current research indicated to these issues.

On the same afternoon, Joe Clarke presented a considerably different view on the topic of discipline and disruptive students. You may remember Clarke, the former principal of Eastside High School in Patterson, New Jersey. The baseball bat-wielding Clarke received national acclaim from former President Reagan for his get-tough approach in cleaning up Eastside High, a tough inner-city high school. Clark threw out all the "troublemakers," excluding from school hundreds of young people. Baseball bat in hand, Clark appeared on the cover of *Time* magazine. He was a guest on *Nightline* and *Donahue*. There even was a popular movie—*Lean On Me*—made about Clark's life and starring Oscar nominee Morgan Freeman. He became a national symbol of the get-tough approach.

I was surprised that Clarke and his get-tough message received such an enthusiastic reception from the school administrators at this Florida conference. I wondered if these administrators really believed that Clarke's approach worked. I doubted that society was better off when all the troublemakers were thrown out of school and onto the streets.

### The Need for Alternative Schools: No Easy Answers to Tough Problems

Joe Clarke, Scared Straight, TOUGH LOVE, as well as many other get-tough proponents and programs share two important characteristics: (a) they present simplistic solutions to complex problems and (b) they usually don't work! There is substantial research that TOUGH LOVE won't make a teenager follow the rules; and that Scared Straight won't prevent a teenager from engaging in acts of juvenile crime. The same argument about getting tough has been raised in regard to criminal behavior and the need for more police on the streets, stricter sentencing guidelines, and the construction of more prisons. Currently, the United States has more than 1 million inmates being held in federal and state prisons. There are an additional 500,000 in county and city jails; 600,000 on parole; 3 million on probation; and 60,000 in juvenile facilities. *In fact, the United States has one of the highest incarceration rates in the world.* In 1971, when statistics on this issue were first compiled, the American imprisonment rate was approximately 100 per 100,000. Today, the rate has soared to 426 per 100,000. Black Americans are 7.8 times more likely to be incarcerated than whites. If present patterns continue, theoretically all black males between 18 and 39 will soon be incarcerated. The costs will be in the hundreds of billions of dollars.

This idea that getting tough works—on crime or difficult adolescents—is perhaps the most pernicious and widely believed idea in the American political arena. Parents are bombarded with messages about the need to take control of their children. In a 1984 speech, former President Ronald Reagan called for a return to "good old fashioned discipline." Reagan said that,

> American schools don't need vast new sums of money as much as they need a few fundamental reforms. First, we need to restore good old-fashioned discipline. . . . We need to write stricter discipline codes; then support our teachers when they enforce those codes. (cited in Gordon, 1989, p. xvii)

The TOUGH LOVE movement urges parents to demand cooperation and vilifies teenagers who misbehave: Wachtel, York, and York (1983) write,

> The common denominator is rotten behavior. Despite a wide range of geographical, social, and economic backgrounds, our young people behave with stereotypical predictability. Like clones stamped out in some satanic laboratory, they share an underlying selfishness and similar ways of demonstrating it. (p. 12)

Bookstores are filled with titles advocating that parents get tough. There are titles such as: *Dare to Discipline, Parent Power, Toughlove,* and *Spank Me If You Love Me.* Numerous polls indicate that parents view discipline as the number one problem in the schools today, with most parents supporting the use of corporal punishment in the schools.

Programs such as Scared Straight (where teenagers visit prisons and are verbally abused and berated by prisoners sentenced to life terms) are promoted as providing a solution to problematic adolescence behavior.

As I will state many time throughout *How to Establish an Alternative School*, though I fully believe in holding young people responsible for their behavior, punitive approaches and programs don't work. Because of the rapidly increasing number of at-risk youth and the fact that punitive approaches don't work, society needs alternative schools.

## Who Should Read This Book

Any parent, teacher, administrator, school board member, social service provider, employee of the juvenile justice system—or any other adult who is involved with at-risk youth—can benefit from reading *How to Establish an Alternative School*. It's important that those involved with at-risk youth become familiar with the kind of comprehensive programs and strategies that are available to help chronically disruptive and disaffected children and adolescents. It's equally important that they become able to distinguish among programs and schools that call themselves "alternative," and realize that the overwhelming majority of alternative schools are alternative in name only, with many representing little more than soft jails.

## The Scope and Treatment of This Book

There are very few comprehensive publications that explain how you can start an effective alternative program. Most of the information that does exist is found in journal articles and focuses on isolated or fragmented issues, such as curriculum, staffing, or counseling. Issues related to the importance of the alternative school site or the political realities of starting an alternative school have for the most part been ignored by writers. In addition to providing a comprehensive approach to the subject, I have taken a decided *organizational development approach* to the material in *How to Establish an Alternative School.*

The success that I have achieved in helping to establish alternative programs is, I believe, to a considerable extent related to my knowledge of organizational design and development. Although I hold an M.A. in Educational Administration and an Ed.D. in Education Leadership, I've found that my M.B.A. in Management and Organizational Development has been more beneficial in my ability to help establish programs for at-risk youth in some of the richest sites (such as college campuses) that America has to offer.

I am convinced that program site is the most important aspect in establishing an effective alternative school. Anyone who has tried to locate on a desirable site a program that serves a difficult population is familiar with the NIMBY (Not In My Backyard) syndrome. The organizational development approach that is emphasized throughout this book will show you how to overcome such resistance through careful planning, management, and public relations activities.

# About the Author

**John Kellmayer** has spent more than 20 years in education, working primarily with chronically disruptive and disaffected students. He holds a B.A. in English from St. Joseph's University; an M.A. in Educational Administration from Rowan State College of New Jersey; an M.B.A. from LaSalle University; and an Ed.D. from Nova Southeastern University. Dr. Kellmayer has taught every grade from fourth through graduate school, has served as an administrator in several schools, including a traditional public high school, a countywide alternative high school, and a school for the emotionally disturbed. In addition, he has worked as a consultant for the New Jersey Department of Education and has taught on the faculties of Penn State and Temple Universities, and Camden County College in Blackwood, New Jersey.

A professional writer with several hundred publications in newspapers, magazines, textbooks, and journals, Dr. Kellmayer's work has appeared in publications such as the *NASSP Bulletin, Educational Digest, Home Life Magazine, Small Business Opportunities Magazine, NJEA Review, Educational Viewpoints, Running Times,* and *Today's Single Parent.*

# 1

## Alternative Education
### What Is It?

*When people ask where I go to high school and I tell them the alternative high school, they almost always ask, "What's an alternative high school?" My parents asked the same question when I started getting in trouble back at the regular high school and the assistant principal recommended that I go to the alternative school. It's difficult to define what an alternative high school really is . . . but there's such a different feeling at the alternative school compared to my old traditional high school. At the alternative school, I feel like I'm important, that the teachers care about me as a person, and that I'm the focus of my own learning experiences. That last part about me being responsible for my own learning experiences can be both kind of scary but kind of cool at the same time.*

*At first I didn't want to attend the alternative school. A lot of people think we're all a bunch of delinquents. But they're so wrong. Sure, some of us have made mistakes, but we're all teenagers. And don't teenagers make mistakes sometimes? Here, we have as strong an academic program as back in the regular high school. But we also have a lot more freedom. That's not to say we're not held responsible for doing the work. It's just how we get the work done can be different. I'm going away to college next year. I think I'll be better prepared because I went to the alternative school . . . more mature and able to handle living on my own. At first, I didn't want to come here. But things weren't working out in regular school. I was getting suspended a lot, cutting classes and failing, and telling off my teachers. Now that I think back, though, with graduation only a couple months away, the alternative school has been one of the best things that ever happened to me.*

—Bob, an 18-year-old senior at a New
Jersey alternative high school

Within the past 20 years, the term *alternative education* has been applied indiscriminantly to such a wide variety of programs that its meaning has been clouded in confusion among educators, students, and the general public. Approximately 2,500 programs that are called "alternative" have been located across the United States. Researchers have estimated that the actual number of alternative schools is probably closer to 5,000.

The term has been attached to magnet schools for subjects such as science, math, and the performing arts; to schools for pregnant teens and teen mothers; to schools-within-schools; to schools without walls; to schools located on college campuses, inside shopping malls, churches, museums, zoos, and amusement parks; to schools for the chronically disruptive, the chronically disaffected, and adjudicated youth; to schools for the intellectually gifted, the emotionally disturbed, and schools for students who require special education; to schools that hold classes during the usual daytime hours, to schools that hold classes in the late afternoon or evening, and to schools that don't hold classes at all.

## Alternatives in Name Only

Despite the thousands of alternative programs throughout the United States, a significant percentage of "alternative" schools are alternative in name only—a point that I will make several times throughout *How to Establish an Alternative School*. These pseudo-alternatives represent ineffective and often punitive approaches that isolate and segregate students who can be difficult from the mainstream. Because of the existence of so many bad alternative programs, the public often perceives *all* alternative programs as second rate—rather than innovative. Many view alternative schools as havens for "misfits" and dumping grounds where difficult adolescents are warehoused.

Gregory (1988) writes,

> Indeed, school people, ever anxious to look like they've engaged in systemic change when they aren't, have effectively sapped the term "alternative" of most any useful denotation. School districts and, in some cases, whole states have warped the term, alternative, to mean school for par-

ticular, usually difficult clientele. Most often, these "alternatives" have become places to send kids, whose behavior has become a constant, embarrassing reminder that today's conventional schools, particularly its secondary schools, are fundamentally flawed enterprises. These new schools are often thinly veiled tracks of their large, unworkable sister schools; they have little autonomy. In some states, it is not very inaccurate to view them as soft jails for adjudicated kids. Misuse of the concept is so widespread that most educators now inextricably link "alternative" with "dis" kids: those whom society has judged disadvantaged, disruptive, or just plain distasteful. (p. 1)

## The Progressive Education Movement of the 1920s and the Social Revolution of the 1960s as the Genesis of Alternative Education

There is disagreement about the origins of alternative education; everyone agrees, however, that alternative schools were not originally established to work with—as Gregory calls them—"dis" kids. Some writers trace the origins of alternative schools to John Dewey and the progressive movement in education in the 1920s. A greater number of writers report that the genesis of the current alternative education movement can be found in the social revolution of the 1960s.

Fizzell (1985) writes,

In the late 1960's, there were three different trends which contributed to the present alternatives. From the civil rights movement came "freedom schools," programs to get away from the racist public schools and to build cultural pride while developing a good education. At about the same time, some middle class liberals began to seek expression of philosophical concerns similar to those of Rousseau and Dewey that the best education is one that is largely under the control of the learner. They established "free schools" in which the students designed their own curriculum and progressed at their own pace. Finally, some educators, concerned with meeting the individual needs of different students, began creating "alternative programs" which provided different learning environments and structures for students who did not "fit in" to the traditional programs. Often these were students who were considered underachievers, unmotivated, or just plain unhappy. (p. 1)

## The Growth of the At-Risk Population and the Transformation of Alternative Programs

As a result of the dramatic increase in school discipline problems that occurred during the past two decades, large numbers of alternative programs have been created to deal with chronically disruptive students. The philosophy that characterizes most of these programs has been markedly different from the philosophy that characterized the initial alternative schools of the 1960s. Too frequently, that philosophy has advocated punishment, isolation, and segregation. As a result, many of today's alternative programs bear little resemblance to earlier humanistic models.

A study conducted by the California Department of Education comparing the major school discipline problems in the 1940s with those of the 1990s illustrates just how much times have changed.

The most common discipline problems of the 1940s included

talking,
chewing gum,
making noise,
running in the hallways,
getting out of place in line,
wearing improper clothing,
not putting paper in wastebaskets.

Compare this list to the problems of the 1990s:

assault,
arson,
rape,
drug and alcohol abuse,

pregnancy,
suicide,
bombings.

The breakdown of the traditional family has also contributed to the dramatic increase in the number of alternative programs. According to the United States census, for every 100 children born today,

48 will be born to parents who divorce.

17 will be born out of wedlock.

16 will be born to parents who separate.

6 will be born to parents, at least one of whom will die before the child will reach 18.

13 will reach age 18 and still be living in a "traditional" family structure.

Also, according to the Children's Defense Fund,

Every 8 seconds an American child drops out of school.

Every 26 seconds a child runs away from home.

Every 47 seconds a child is abused and neglected.

Every 67 seconds a teenager has a baby.

Every 7 minutes an adolescent is arrested for a drug offense.

Every 30 minutes an adolescent is arrested for drunken driving.

Every 53 minutes a child dies.

Teen suicide is at an all-time high.

Teen abortion is at an all-time high.

As a result of the social disintegration of the past two decades, alternative programs also began to serve a chronically disaffected population. Today, we refer to chronically disruptive and chronically disaffected students as "at risk." A great many of the new alternative schools have been designed to work with this at-risk population. Mintz (1994) writes,

There has been a gradual increase in the number of alternatives founded each year, starting with a low ebb in the early fifties. After reaching an initial peak in the late sixties and early seventies, there was a slight dip. But starting in the late seventies there has been a dramatic *increase* in foundings of educational alternatives, with over 60% of them founded since the early eighties. Without much fanfare, this movement has been growing much faster than many people would have believed. (p. 5)

## Do Programs for At-Risk Students Represent Real Alternatives?

If you read the literature on alternative education, you'll discover that many authorities do not consider programs for at-risk students to represent *real alternatives*. The rationale behind their reasoning is that most of these programs are punitive in nature, do not represent any significant (positive) difference from the mainstream, and that students and staff are often assigned to such programs against their will. Although I agree with those who argue that punitive programs do not represent real alternatives, I feel they are mistaken when they state that programs for at-risk youth cannot be considered real alternatives. In fact, *I would strongly argue that it is the population of at-risk students that is most in need of real alternative programs.*

I don't wish to become involved in a philosophical discussion concerning the almost innumerable meanings that have been attached to the phrase *alternative education*. If you're interested in such a discussion, you can find this information in several of the articles listed in the Resource Sections of *How to Establish an Alternative School*. I am, however, going to make several assumptions regarding the reasons that you bought this book.

1. Your school or district has been experiencing a problem in meeting the needs of a distinct population of students— whether they are disruptive, disaffected, gifted, or some other group of students who have not responded to a traditional school program.

2. You are interested in creating an alternative program that will address the needs of this population of students.

3. You want to create the most effective program that you can, within the constraints of your resources.

4. You sincerely care about helping adolescents—no matter how difficult their behavior may sometimes be—as opposed to punishing, isolating, or segregating them.

## Classification Systems and Alternative Programs

Raywid (1990) has established a classification system that seems to encompass all types of alternative programs, from the most humanistic through the most punitive. Raywid (1990) classifies alternative programs into one of three types:

There are still people trying to design new schools, and they are responsible for what I call Type 1 alternatives: programs designed in answer to the search for an education that will simultaneously prove more humane, more responsive, more challenging, and more compelling for all involved. Type 2 alternatives are often judgmental in posture and punitive in orientation. This is what might be expected from an alternative school whose self-reported distinction lies in removing disruptive youngsters to leave others to study in peace. Such programs have been called "soft jails," and indeed there is reason for doing so. Their students are assigned to them— often as a last chance proposition just prior to expulsion— and instead of the "liberation" theme of the early alternative schools, there are likely to be highly structured, tightly regulated and supervised programs that are expected to employ behavior correction strategies, along with firm and aggressive disciplinary policies. Still a third variety of alternative schools has developed, whose guiding metaphor appears to be therapy rather than reform school. . . . These programs are clearly more humanistic in orientation than Type 2 alternatives, but they share with Type 2 programs at least one critical assumption, namely, it is that the cause of the student's troubles lies somewhere within the student. The difficulty is not that the student needs a different *kind* of education, or that there is a bad match between school and youngster; it is that the youngster is flawed in some important respect. They thus construe their mission as helping to eliminate the flaw—a matter of intensive counseling, or unusual support, or remediation. Most typically, the focus is on changing behavior or attitudes, and the therapy component dominated the program—with the result that academic instruction often takes a back seat (at least on-grade-level instruction) and there is rarely much staff attention given to rethinking instruction or curriculum. (p. 25)

Other writers have suggested that programs can be classified according to one of the following four components.

1. *Location:* for example, a school within-a-school; an after school program; a school in a shopping mall; a school on a college campus; a school without walls; and so forth.
2. *The Nature of the Program:* for example, Raywid's classification scheme divides alternative programs into one of three types, ranging from punitive to humanistic.
3. *The Problems or Discrepancies the Program Has Been Created to Address:* for example, a school for disruptive students; a school for disaffected students; a school for adjudicated students; a school for pregnant teens and teen parents; a magnet school created around a particular subject, such as the performing arts, science, math, or the environment. (Rather than limiting a program to a specific population, some successful schools serve various populations.)
4. *The Student Needs That the Program Has Been Created to Address:* for example, cognitive or perceptual needs; affective or social needs; or time-related needs (the need for a more flexible schedule).

## A Comment About Alternative Programs at the Elementary and Middle School Level

As you read *How to Establish an Alternative School,* you may feel that the book is disproportionately oriented toward programs at the 9-12 level. Despite the need for early intervention, there are very few separate and distinct alternative schools that operate at the elementary school level. Though there are more "true" alternative programs at the middle school level, the number of alternative middle school programs is still quite small. Many districts have developed programs of diagnosis and early identification of kindergarten and elementary school students. For the most part, however, methods to help at-risk students on the K-8 level consist of "Band-Aid" approaches, such as full day kindergarten or the availability of extra tutoring or counseling services. In later chapters, I'll make suggestions concerning the development of full-fledged alternative programs at the elementary and middle school levels for students who are potentially at risk.

## So What Is Alternative Education?

There are probably as many different definitions of alternative education as there are alternative programs. Some writers view alternative education in an almost revolutionary manner. For example, Miller (1994) believes that,

> Alternative education is genuinely countercultural—it yearns to replace those values and assumptions that have dominated Western, particularly American, culture over the past two or three centuries. Its vision is profoundly humane, person-centered, democratic, and attuned to the deep human quest for meaning and purpose. For the most part, this vision has remained on the fringes of American education and society, but given the crisis in modern education, a progressive social and educational movement that draws inspiration from its own rich heritage could have a profound impact on our thinking about schooling and learning. (p. 28)

Other writers, such as Kozol, see alternative programs as an expression of society's idealism. Kozol writes,

> The Free School [or Alternative School] was conceived, not as an instrument by which to flee from history, but rather as a visible metaphor for many values, visions, and ideals that seemed to some of us to be essential in the struggle to assure the psychological and intellectual survival of our children. (cited in Mintz, 1994, p. 14)

Students like Bob, the New Jersey senior who attends an alternative high school and who's quoted at the beginning of this chapter, view alternative programs as places where they have much greater freedom and opportunities for choices than in a traditional school.

I'm not going to attempt to define what alternative education is or is not. Instead, *How to Establish an Alternative School* will show you how to set up an effective alternative school that can dramatically change the direction of young lives. And I believe that's why most readers bought this book. If you're a teacher or administrator who's considering establishing your own alternative program, *How to Establish an Alternative School* will provide you with the information to establish a cost-effective program that will meet the needs of both the traditional school or district, as well as those students who will attend your new alternative program. Although the very nature of alternative education makes it difficult to provide a step-by-step blueprint for establishing a new program, the principles explained in this book provide the foundation upon which you can build an alternative school that works.

# 2

# Dealing With Political Opposition
# and Credibility Gaps

*"Alternative schools are dumping grounds for bad kids."*
*"Kids are warehoused at alternative schools."*
*"Kids at alternative schools get away with murder."*
*"There are no standards at alternative schools. They give credits away
    there."*
*"Alternative programs cost too much money."*
*"Alternative schools reward bad behavior."*
*"I would never send my child to an alternative school. They're second-rate
    programs."*
*"If they can't make it here, why should we pay for them to go to an
    alternative school?"*
*"Those alternative programs are havens for outcasts, misfits, and losers."*

Over the years I've heard hundreds of statements like these, which illustrate the controversial nature of alternative programs. The sad fact is that for many alternative programs, comments such as these are absolutely valid. Many people equate alternative with second rate, rather than innovative. Alternative programs have a bad reputation, in part, because many of these programs *deserve* a bad reputation.

11

It's not surprising that alternative programs tend to be controversial and to have a bad reputation. As I point out several times in this book, a great many of these programs are alternative in name only and are in reality "soft jails" designed to isolate difficult students from the mainstream. Unfortunately, the mind-set of many of those in positions of authority to create alternative programs is such that punitive programs are common. I'll never forget a time when I was giving a presentation on the need for more alternative programs to a large group of school superintendents. I made a remark that we needed schools where students were free to work out their personal and emotional problems (and the concomitant behavioral problems that accompany this problem-solving process) without risking automatic suspension or expulsion as a consequence of such behaviors. A superintendent of two large high schools interrupted my presentation and said, "We have those kinds of places already. They're called prisons." The superintendent laughed hard at his own remark.

Regardless of the kind of alternative program you intend to design, you're going to have to learn to deal with political opposition and credibility gaps. If you design a nonpunitive, innovative, or experiential program for difficult students, you'll hear comments like, "You're rewarding bad behavior." (My response is always that we reward changed behavior.) If you award credits based upon some standard other than the Carnegie unit, you'll be criticized for "giving away credits." If you allow students to call you by your first name, you'll be criticized for "not demanding respect from students."

Throughout the years I've heard my students called animals (I've been called the zoo keeper); criminals (I've been called the warden); and mental cases (I've been called the head psychiatrist). One of the alternative programs I've been principal of was located on a college campus. I remember one instance when a college administrator witnessed a female student curse and scream at me for several minutes. At the height of her outburst, the girl tried to take a swing at me. I reacted very calmly to the girl's tirade, averted her punch, and tried to calm her down. I did not punish her for the outburst.

Afterwards, I learned that the college administrator who had witnessed the exchange had written a letter to my superintendent and to the county superintendent of schools. The letter stated that I was a disgrace as a principal, that my students had no respect for me, and that they were allowed to get away with murder. The administrator wrote that it was time for me to "get tough" with the students.

What the college administrator who had witnessed the exchange did not know was that girl had a serious substance abuse problem and had recently witnessed her mother's suicide. (Her mother had been in great pain due to terminal cancer.) I wonder, had he known about this student's background, if that college administrator would have still believed that punishment was an appropriate response, rather than the counseling that the girl received.

Assuming that you succeed in designing an effective and high-quality program, you must learn to live with criticism from those who won't understand or who will doubt what you're trying to accomplish. You must learn to respond to their criticism in a positive and professional manner; you must explain the rationale behind your program design, educate critics as to the proper way to deal with difficult students, and continually publicize your successes. You must make your program credible, even in the eyes of your critics.

Bierlein and Vandergrift (1993) write,

> There is a credibility issue surrounding alternative schools. Many non-alternative school staff view alternative programs as offering an "easy out" for students who have not suc-ceeded in the mainstream. Therefore, high academic stand-ards and quality curriculum must be in place for an alterna-tive school to have a positive effect. (p. 5)

## Relationships With Larger System(s)

It is imperative that the alternative program maintain a positive relationship with the parent school or schools, as well as those additional agencies and organizations with which the program is involved. Ironically, maintaining a positive relationship with the parent school or schools (which often created the impetus for the program in the first place) is generally more difficult than maintain-ing positive relations with other agencies or organizations.

### Conflicts With the Alternative School Site

Alternative programs, particularly those that work with at-risk students, often come into conflict with the host site. In order to avoid conflict with the host site (or school), a great many alternative programs are located at sites that tend to segregate students from the mainstream; or meet at times when alternative school students cannot come in contact with the mainstream. This conflict with the host site (or school) also frequently results in a punitive program orientation. Although the desire to avoid conflict with the host site is understandable, a certain amount of conflict is inevitable and a necessary by-product of the change process that occurs in students. *Conflict with the host site should be managed, not avoided.*

If you establish a program for disruptive students and experience no conflict with the host site, it is likely that you are working with disaffected students rather than disruptive students. There are many programs throughout the United States that purport to be helping disruptive students, when, in fact, they are actually working with a disaffected population. Though these programs are fulfilling an important function, they are impacting drop-out rates instead of juvenile delinquency rates.

What is the cause of this conflict? To a large measure, the answer to this question depends upon the site of the alternative program. In general, the richer the alternative program site, the more powerful is the effect of the site on modifying students' academic and affective performance. Conversely, the more powerful the effect of the site on modifying students' academic and affective performance, the greater the level of cultural clash that results when students from the alternative program come in close contact with students (or other individuals) from the host school or site.

The following two examples illustrate how alternative programs can come in conflict with the host school or site. (Issues related to site will be discussed in detail in Chapter 4.)

*School-Within-a-School.* A very common model, the school-within-a-school alternative program is typically located in a wing of a traditional school building. Problems often arise because the traditional program and the alternative program invariably have different sets of rules. The inability of students to comply with the rules of a traditional program is one of the most common reasons for students being placed in an alternative program in the first place. Although the programs are located in separate areas of the same school building, students from the alternative program frequently come in contact (and conflict) with students and staff from the traditional program.

An issue then arises whether alternative school students should be dealt with differently than students who attend the traditional school. As a result of this conflict, the alternative program may acquire a bad reputation. Also, in order to minimize the extent of this conflict, alternative programs located within the same building with the passage of time tend to resemble a smaller version of the traditional program and to become punitively oriented. Because of conflicts with the host site, I know of many instances when full-time day alternative programs that operated in a wing of a traditional school were changed to after school or evening programs, thus further isolating troubled students from the mainstream.

*College-Based Model.* An extremely powerful model, college-based alternative programs integrate at-risk high school students into the adult environment of the college campus. The college-based model was established on the belief that the socialization effect that results from this integration will produce substantial cognitive and affective growth among alternative school students and serve as a "slingshot" for upward social mobility. Here, it is not so much two sets of rules that come in conflict; rather, it is two cultures. Because of pressures on the alternative program to reduce the extent of this cultural clash, college-based alternative schools tend to "soften" the population over time. Many of these programs, which originally were established to work with disruptive students, wind up working only with disaffected students.

One of the nation's first and largest college-based programs is located on the campus of LaGuardia Community College in New York City. The LaGuardia program is called Middle College High School.

Lieberman (1985) writes,

Another intangible problem results from the societal attitude toward teenagers as a subculture. At the outset of the experience, Middle College students were blamed for every problem encountered by the institution. When the sprinkler system went off accidentally, it was the high school's fault. Gradually, the principals worked with the security and maintenance staff to educate them and make them allies in our mission. Now the head of security, a former policeman, teaches law and justice to Middle College as an adjunct for high school credit, which prepares the students for higher education. . . . To make a "mesh" of programs, administrators need to recognize that the two educational settings represent distinct cultures. (p. 7)

Lieberman writes about the need to make a "mesh" of the high school and college programs. In order to achieve such a mesh, the administrator and staff must develop a keen understanding of the college culture. Adopting the methods of the ethnographer can assist the administrator and faculty in successfully integrating the alternative school culture into the culture of the host site.

Wagner (1989) compares an effective school administrator to an ethnographer:

As a template for identifying parallels between the work of ethnographers and school administrators, let me define ethnography to include those perspectives and methods associated with anthropology and sociology through which researchers try to develop an understanding of (a) how a group or people live and work together, (b) the meanings those people either construct or perceive in the activities they share, and (c) the practices through which they affirm, refine, or give life to such meaning. Let me further propose that the goals of ethnographic perspectives and methods are to develop clear, communicable understandings and interpretations of human behavior within specific contexts of social and cultural activity. Not only do schools and schooling represent contexts in which such understanding and interpretation are frequently at issue, but specific educational practices are constructed out of social interaction guided by such interpretations. (p. 22)

I had similar experiences when I established a countywide alternative high school for chronically disruptive and disaffected secondary students on the campus of Atlantic Community College in Mays Landing, New Jersey. Although as principal of this alternative high school I had many duties, my most important responsibility was to manage (and minimize the extent of) the cultural clash that resulted from the integration of the two cultures.

The management of this cultural clash is essentially a political process. If the administrator of the alternative program fails to effectively manage this political process, the program may be closed, or the program may become something that it was not originally intended to be (shift from disruptive to disaffected students or some other "softer" population). As part of this process, the alternative school administrator must become aware of the culture and norms of the host site.

## Managing the Political Process and Political Controversies

The most important component of the political process is to involve in the program members of all major constituent groups that are impacted or affected by the alternative school. This includes members of groups that may be opposed to the alternative program. The extent of this involvement must be determined by the alternative school administrator. For example, at Atlantic Community College I established a clearinghouse that reviewed all discipline decisions that I made in instances that involved alternative school students and college personnel (including college students) and property. The clearinghouse consisted of the college dean of students and representatives from the college faculty, college security, and college physical plant. Although the responsibility for administering discipline was mine and mine alone, the clearinghouse, which functioned in a manner similar to a civilian/police review board, added credibility among the college community regarding my discipline decisions. As a result of the clearinghouse and the credibility it brought me in the eyes of the college community, I was allowed considerable latitude in dealing with chronically disruptive students. There were times that alternative school students became involved in fights with college students, damaged college property, or in some other way negatively impacted the college. Because the clearinghouse was familiar with the difficult background and potentials of these students, it generally approved of my decisions. More importantly, I was not pressured or forced to dismiss students who had adversely impacted—sometimes seriously—the college. This is what I mean by managing conflict rather than attempting to avoid it entirely by turning a program into something that it was not originally intended to be.

### Public Relations and Marketing

Similarly, I established a college advisory committee that provided input on curriculum, facilitated college personnel serving as guest speakers in high school classes, worked with high school faculty in writing grant proposals, and similar kinds of projects that proved mutually beneficial to both the high school and college. In addition, a student service club that performed volunteer work both on and off campus was established. Students participated in unpaid campus internships in which they were paired with college faculty or staff. Also, a peer mentor program that paired alternative school students with college students was created. A newsletter that publicized the alternative high school's successes was published every month. Area newspapers were contacted, and reporters visited the alternative high school and wrote favorable stories on the program. Although it's helpful to promote your school in print (newsletters, press releases, etc.), it's more effective to create programs that will foster close, positive, and continuing contacts among alternative school students and members of the host site.

Assuming that you succeed in designing a quality program, most of the students in your alternative program should be successful over time. Promote their successes as much as possible. Don't allow the failure or problems created by a few students to create negative publicity about the entire program.

I could list many more strategies that we used to fully integrate alternative high school students into the college environment. What is important to note, however, is that I viewed marketing and public relations as a function as important as budgeting, program planning, and curriculum development. Just as the alternative high school teachers took attendance every day, I engaged in some form of marketing and public relations activities *every single day*.

When the alternative high school was established on the campus of Atlantic Community College, a substantial majority of the college community was opposed to the program and did not believe that a high school for chronically disruptive students should be established on campus. In fact, the first that anyone on campus learned about the proposed alternative program was a story that appeared in the largest county newspaper about a month before the school opened. The headline of the story stated, "ACC to Take Unruly Students." Talk about your rough starts.

For the first few years, the survival of the school was seriously in doubt. Because of the usual kinds of behaviors that at-risk students engage in, several influential college professors and administrators lobbied to have the program thrown off campus. A distinct "us against them" mentality developed. To change this mentality, I embarked upon an extensive needs assessment to determine the predominant attitudes and values of the college toward the alternative school. This needs assessment included in-depth interviews with 50 college administrators, faculty, and staff who had been identified as opinion leaders on campus.

I also studied the college culture, including the formal and informal college organization. Based upon the results of this needs assessment, a multifaceted intervention plan (including public relations activities) was formulated. Around the 4th or 5th year, I realized that an important perceptual change had occurred and that my intervention plan was proving effective. Many college personnel, including faculty and staff that had formerly opposed the program, began referring to the students as "our kids." My strategies had succeeded, and the college embraced the program as an important part of the college community. Because of the success of my intervention plan, the NIMBY (Not In My Backyard) Syndrome—which prevents many programs that serve difficult populations from locating in rich environments—had been overcome.

## Other Sources of Potential Conflict With the Parent School

Regardless of the site of the alternative program, conflicts with the home school can also arise over any number of additional issues. These issues should be worked out cooperatively and prior to the start of the alternative program by members of the alternative school staff and the parent school administration. A few of these issues follow.

*Credit Awarding.* Many students who attend an alternative program have fallen behind in credits. It is not unusual to find 16-, 17-, or 18-year-old freshmen enrolled in an alternative school. In order to provide these students with an opportunity to accumulate additional credits, you'll need to permit students to earn credits based upon proficiency, as well as the traditional time-based method of awarding credits (the Carnegie Unit). Most states allow all public schools to award credits on the basis of proficiency, though few traditional programs utilize this option. In general, you may award credits based upon proficiency in one of two ways:

1. Successful performance on a comprehensive exam or series of exams in a given subject area.
2. Successful completion of an independent study project or course. The exam or project should in some manner test or include content that is comparable to what would be covered in a traditional time-based course. In each case, a complete record of the exam or independent study project should be maintained.

Be careful about awarding credit based upon proficiency. It's important that credit not be given away. At the same time, however, don't be reluctant to award an unusually high number of credits to a student if the student really completes the work. If you award an unusually high number of credits to an alternative school student and that same student earned few or no credits while attending a traditional school, you may be criticized by individuals in the parent school. It's important, therefore, to maintain adequate documentation regarding the awarding of credit based upon proficiency. Also, be creative in designing alternative examinations, assignments, and projects through which students can earn proficiency-based credits.

*Attendance.* Depending upon how rigorous the attendance requirements of the parent school may be, you may need to work out a more flexible attendance policy for the alternative program. Many students who attend alternative schools have unusual living arrangements (the necessity of taking care of small children) or other circumstances (the necessity of working) that may prevent them from attending school on the same schedule as students in a traditional program. Rather than following the same attendance policy as the traditional program, special arrangements should be made for those students with such circumstances. Such students could be placed on a combination time-based and proficiency-based program, or even a 100% proficiency-based program.

*Participation in Home School Activities.* If a student from the alternative school wishes to participate in extracurricular activities held at the home school, permission should be granted on a case-by-case basis by the parent school administrator, following consultation with the alternative school administrator. Students should not be categorically excluded from such events.

*Discipline Matters.* For the most serious incidents (e.g., substance abuse or weapons offenses), I would recommend that the alternative program follow the identical rules as followed by the parent school. For less serious incidents, however, the alternative school administrator should have substantial discretion in deciding appropriate discipline. To illustrate, let's suppose the traditional school policy calls for automatic suspension for a student who fights another student or curses out a teacher.

Because many students who attend alternative programs have had difficulty in complying with traditional rules, the alternative school administrator should decide the most appropriate course of action, rather than simply going "by the book." Requiring students who fight to participate in peer mediation or undergoing counseling may do them a lot more good than being suspended out of school.

## Conclusions

In order to deal effectively with political opposition and credibility gaps, you need to remember only three basic points.

1. Establish a quality program.
2. Continuously involve members of all significant constituent groups in the operation of the alternative program.
3. Make marketing and public relations high priorities and activities that you do every day.

# 3

# Ten Key Characteristics of Effective Alternative Programs

As I explained in the first chapter, more than 2,500 programs that are called "alternative" are located across the United States. Though many—perhaps most—of these programs are alternative in name only, a significant number of effective alternative programs have existed for a long enough period of time that researchers have been able to determine the key characteristics of effective programs. If you're considering establishing an alternative program, keep in mind that a new program does not necessarily have to demonstrate all these components in its first few years. In fact, a few of these program elements—such as issues related to school culture—can only be developed over a period of years. The important point is to work to ensure that your alternative program eventually incorporates all the components that characterize effective programs. Most of these components are discussed in greater detail in separate chapters of *How to Establish an Alternative School*.

## 1. Size

If you review some of the articles listed in the Sources for More Information section at the end of *How to Establish an Alternative School*, you'll find repeated references to the concept that smaller size makes for a better alternative program. For example, across the United States there are thousands of small programs that serve between 10 and 50 students. Considering the other characteristics of effective alternative programs that are discussed in this chapter, it makes absolute sense that smaller is better. For example, it's much easier to foster a family atmosphere, provide for individualized learning opportunities, and promote participatory decision making when enrollment is limited to fewer than 50 students.

At the same time, however, I'm convinced that it is to a large measure *because* of small size that so many alternative programs fail to become institutionalized and so pass out of existence. The history of alternative education is filled with programs that have survived for only a few years and then were closed. I've been consulted by many districts—or consortiums of districts—that have been interested in starting alternative programs. Assuming that these districts have a need for a larger program, I advise them that *within reasonable limits*, "to become as big as you can as fast as you can." The idea is simple—larger programs assume a greater organizational identity and are much more difficult to eliminate.

There are two distinct problems that come with bigger programs: (a) they are more difficult to manage; and (b) because of organizational dynamics, they tend to become more traditionally structured.

Larger alternative programs, therefore, are more likely to survive. You should also be aware that over time, all alternative programs—large or small—tend to become more traditionally structured. Those administering larger alternative programs must continually work to ensure that the alternative program does not become simply a smaller version of a large traditional program. A few hundred students (perhaps selected from a consortium of districts) would seem to represent the maximum size of the very largest alternative program. For most programs, 100-125 students may represent the maximum advisable enrollment. Those programs with fewer than 50 or 60 students are much more likely to be closed because of political, financial, or other issues over which the alternative program exercises little control.

A curious side-effect related to greater size is the impact of program size on student behavior. Contrary to what is commonly believed, I have found that student discipline tends to improve when smaller alternative programs accept more students. With a very small group (20-30 students), behavioral norms are not as powerful an influence as with a larger group. Also, with a smaller group, administrators—concerned with their program becoming too small or being eliminated entirely—are often reluctant to dismiss students because of an egregious offense or poor attendance. With a larger group, however (and when there is a large group there is often a waiting list of additional students who wish to enter the alternative program), administrators are more likely to dismiss students who commit particularly serious discipline offenses or who rarely attend school. As a result, students attending larger alternative programs understand that if they do not take advantage of the opportunity to attend an alternative school, they may be dismissed and replaced by other students who will appreciate that opportunity.

## 2. Site

Although the importance of site—and site is of *great importance*—will be discussed in detail in Chapter 4, as a general principle: the richer the site, the more effective the program. Unfortunately, given the stigma that is sometimes attached to alternative programs, many of the "richest" sites (college campuses, for instance) are reluctant to open their doors to these programs, especially those programs that accept more difficult students. At a minimum, students should have access to computers and other forms of technology, science laboratories, counseling and employment services, and recreational facilities. Cost-per-pupil should be about the same as for students who attend a traditional program. In other words, students attending alternative programs should have access to the same level of academic and support services that they would have received had they remained in a traditional school environment.

An important concept related to site involves the socioeconomic status (SES) of alternative program students and the SES of the predominant culture where the alternative program is located. One of the most important and comprehensive studies ever undertaken concerning student achievement in America's public schools was the Equality of Educational Opportunity Report (Coleman et al., 1966; also known as the Coleman Report), which was commissioned by the United States Congress in 1966.

According to the Equality of Educational Opportunity Report (Coleman et al., 1966),

Schools bring little influence to bear on a child's achievement that is independent of his background and general social context; and this very lack of an independent effect means that the inequalities imposed on children by their home, neighborhood, and peer environment are carried along to become the inequalities with which they confront adult life at the end of school. For equality of educational opportunity through the schools must imply a strong effect of schools that is independent of the child's immediate social environment, and that strong independent effect is not present in American schools. (p. 325)

The Equality of Educational Opportunity Report (Coleman et al., 1966) also states that, "The social composition of the student body is more highly related to achievement, independently of the student's own background, than is any school factor" (p. 325). This report stresses the importance of socioeconomic status and the environment in which learning takes place on student achievement. Because many students who attend alternative programs come from backgrounds characterized by low parental SES, if the alternative program can be situated in a site that can somehow integrate students from a lower SES background with students or nonstudents from a higher SES background, the effect on students' cognitive and affective development can be powerful. Unfortunately, this kind of integration is very rare in alternative programs. Much more commonly, alternative programs—in an effort to avoid this integration and the cultural clash that results from the integration—are located in sites or operate during hours that act to isolate (rather than to integrate) students.

Because it is often difficult to establish alternative programs in some of the most desirable sites, you may wish to establish your program in a less desirable site, with the idea of eventually moving the program to a more desirable location.

## 3. Voluntarism

As much as possible, participation in the alternative program should be voluntary for both students and staff. Especially in the case of staff, teachers should not be assigned to a program in which they do not wish to teach. Nor should issues such as contract rights and "bumping" privileges be allowed to control decisions related to the alternative program teaching staff. I'm familiar with several excellent alternative programs that were adversely impacted (and eventually closed) because declining enrollment in the parent school district led to teacher layoffs. Exercising seniority rights, teachers who were ill-suited to work with an alternative population and who did not wish to teach in an alternative program replaced teachers who had been successful in the alternative program.

Teachers in alternative programs must be well trained in human relations and understand the important distinction between *influence* and *control*. You gain more influence over teenagers the less you try to control them. Conversely, the more that you try to control teenagers—especially the kind of difficult adolescents who often wind up in alternative programs—the less real influence you have over them. Teachers who do not understand and accept this premise do not belong in an alternative program.

The issue of voluntarism becomes much more complicated with regard to students. Many researchers have stated that students should not be forced to attend an alternative program. At the same time, however, alternative programs often represent the last chance for chronically disruptive and disaffected students who have been unsuccessful in a traditional program. School administrators, therefore, may have no choice except to assign a chronically disruptive student to an alternative program. I have known hundreds of situations where a student who had committed an egregious act (a weapons offense, for example) while attending a traditional program has been assigned to an alternative program in lieu of expulsion. In fact, I have personally assigned chronically disruptive students to *nonpunitive* alternative programs. Most of these students later thanked me for the opportunity to attend an alternative program.

Mary Ellen Sweeney and Ann Wheelock (1989) write,

> Clearly educators, advocates, and parents must oppose alternatives which are based on segregation and exclusion. Some of these programs are punitive in nature, designed to separate disruptive students from the mainstream until it is decided that they can conform to the mainstream. Others are considered remedial, designed to help students catch up so they can reenter traditional classrooms. However, experience indicated that students' gains resulting from either of

these models are temporary and that the problems recur once students are back in the situation that may have contributed to the initial problem. (p. 6)

I agree with Sweeney and Wheelock that programs that exclude students from the mainstream because of behavioral or academic problems should be opposed. Nevertheless, a sizable percentage of all alternative programs result in just that: separation or exclusion. This illustrates a point that I make throughout *How to Establish an Alternative School*—that a significant majority of all programs that are called alternative are, in fact, alternative in name only.

If you intend to establish an alternative program for chronically disruptive students and to assign students to this program, make every effort to create a nonpunitive model that is as rich as or even richer than the traditional school program from which students have been excluded. *Punitive models are ineffective for all students—whether disruptive or not.* Even the claims made by supporters of the most punitive kinds of models, boot camps for example, are specious. For it has been clearly demonstrated that punitive programs do not produce lasting cognitive or affective development. If you want to create a punitive program, a "soft jail" that is designed to simply warehouse adolescents and keep them isolated from the mainstream, then call it that. But don't use the term *alternative*. It is because so many of these soft jails exist and call themselves alternative, that real alternative programs are often unfairly characterized as havens for misfits and delinquents. (Suggestions for establishing effective and nonpunitive alternative models are provided in Chapter 4.)

Also, you should realize that if your efforts to create a true alternative prove successful, then the great majority of students (including those who were assigned to the program against their will) will *not* wish to leave the program and return to the mainstream after they have been "cured." Many alternative programs operate on the erroneous assumption that after a certain period of time in the program, students will want to return to a traditional program. This is only the case if the alternative program is perceived by students as punitive or inferior to the traditional program. Remember that alternative does not have to mean inferior. In the good programs, it means "superior."

Furthermore, if you are working with an at-risk population, to return students to the mainstream is to invite a perpetuation of previous failures and problems. Students who attend the most effective alternative programs generally graduate from the program, receiving the same diploma as students who attend the parent school. These students usually believe that they are receiving a superior education in the alternative school setting. For example, in the college-based model, alternative school students are generally permitted to take college courses on a tuition-free basis. Theoretically, it's possible for an at-risk student who attends a college-based alternative school to be simultaneously awarded a high school diploma and college degree.

Related to the idea of return to the traditional school is the issue of program size. In the best alternative programs, students rarely choose to return to the traditional school. I have, however, known cases where students were forced against their will to return to a traditional school after having experienced success in an alternative program. Students have been forced to return to a traditional program because a limited number of positions were available in the alternative program and another student was deemed more in need. *I consider this practice to be unconscionable.*

Because students should be allowed to remain in the alternative program until graduation, there will be an impetus to steadily increase enrollment so that other at-risk students may be admitted. Another impetus to increase enrollment will come from alternative students who have friends who have previously dropped out of a traditional school and who wish to return to the alternative program.

The following advice may seem paradoxical; however, I think you'll see my point. In Chapter 2, I write about the need to publicize alternative programs effectively. Let me caution you, however, about promoting your program *to students* if you are unable to accept additional students. At one of the alternative schools I administered, I was frequently asked if we had a brochure to describe our program and services. I resisted the idea of a brochure for one simple reason. The program was so successful that our waiting list consisted of several hundred students. I did not wish to publicize a program, raise the hopes of prospective students, and then inform them that there was no space. It's critical to promote your program to all major constituencies, boards, organizations, and agencies with which the program is involved. At the same time, however, the good alternative programs don't have to do much promoting to prospective students. Word of mouth from current students to prospective students takes care of that.

## 4. Participatory Decision Making

Various models of democratic all-school governance systems allow students and staff to have a real voice in the day-to-day operation of the alternative program. Similarly, parents and the community should be involved in program planning and operation.

Gordon (1991), founder of P.E.T. (Parent Effectiveness Training) and T.E.T. (Teacher Effectiveness Training), writes,

> When children are given the opportunity to participate in determining policies and in setting rules, several good things happen. Children feel better about themselves, have higher self-esteem and self-confidence. Most important, they feel they have gained more "fate control"—more personal control over their own lives. They also feel they are equal members of the family, classroom, or school, with an equal voice in making decisions and establishing rules—they're part of a team, not second class citizens. This means that families and classrooms that function collaboratively and democratically will have closer and warmer relationships than those in which the adults act as bosses or authorities expect the children to obey the rules made for them. (p. 147)

Student advisory councils should be formed to allow a mechanism for students to provide input into the governance of the alternative program. Depending on the skills and interests of the student advisory council, students could provide input into a wide range of issues, including matters related to discipline, acceptance of new students, curriculum, field trips, and even staffing. The formation of an effective student council program can be a difficult proposition when working with at-risk students. Because many at-risk students lack effective social or interpersonal skills, they may struggle to function successfully in groups. It's ironic, but I've seen shouting matches and even fights break out the first time some alternative programs have tried to bring students together to establish a peer mediation program or student advisory council.

As a result of previous behavior problems, most at-risk students have had only limited opportunity to participate in group activities or to practice higher order thinking skills. Sadly, at-risk students often think of work that requires discussion, cooperation, and the use of higher order thinking as not "real work." They may complain about teachers who attempt to engage them in such activities, saying that, "We don't do any real work in there. We just sit around and talk about stupid stuff that nobody cares about." These students may find it difficult to stay on task throughout the class period. They may disrupt the entire class or put their heads down on the desk and sleep. Ironically, if the teacher distributes a "find-a-word" puzzle or shows a movie or video, these same students will stop disrupting the class. This reflects the lamentable fact that many teachers of disruptive students had previously attempted to pacify them with non-challenging, low-level cognitive assignments. In traditional programs, some teachers of difficult students try to negotiate an unwritten "truce" with students— "You don't bother me, and I won't bother you."

During my first year of teaching, I did something like this myself. I volunteered to supervise an after school detention hall in a traditional public high school. Every afternoon for one full school year, I supervised an auditorium filled with about 75 of the most difficult students in the high school. The assistant principal, whose interpersonal skills left something to be desired, would periodically enter the auditorium and yell at students for offenses such as talking quietly to each other or wearing hats. In return, some of these students would curse or threaten the assistant principal, thereby precipitating a major incident that usually ended with the student being suspended out of school for several days. Because the assistant principal was not going to change the way in which he related to students, I devised a plan to pacify the students and appease the assistant principal. I allowed students either to work on homework assignments (few did, however), sleep, or complete find-a-word puzzles, which they absolutely loved. I would buy find-a-word puzzle books, make copies of the puzzles, and distribute them to students in detention hall.

I was both amazed and appalled at how diligently they worked on their puzzles. (I ran this detention hall in the late 1970s, and students would spend the whole 45 minutes searching for *Led Zeppelin* in the find-the-rock-group puzzle.) I would also allow students to talk quietly to each other, with the stipulation that when the assistant principal entered the auditorium they would stop talking.

Despite the difficulties involved in engaging at-risk students in group activities and higher-order thinking skills, efforts must be made in this direction. Effective alternative programs challenge students intellectually.

## 5. Curriculum

Successful alternative programs attempt to achieve many of the same academic goals as do traditional programs. It is *how* alternative and traditional programs attempt to achieve these goals that differentiate them in regard to curriculum. The alternative program curriculum should be student-centered, and instruction should be related to students' personal concerns. Many students will attempt to earn credits on the basis of proficiency. Portfolio assessment is particularly useful in awarding credit based upon proficiency. Many alternative programs also award academic credit to students who hold down part-time employment or perform community service activities. A member of the alternative school staff should visit the student on the job site and monitor his work performance and hours. Students do not necessarily have to leave school early to participate in this program. Students who work evenings and weekends are also eligible to earn credits through this option.

It's also important to remember that for students who attend alternative programs affective development often precedes cognitive development. Mary Anne Raywid (1988), who has published extensively on matters related to alternative education, writes that,

> An alternative must have broad aims, making its concern the full development of each youngster—character and intellect, personal and social development, as well as academic achievement. It is concerned with the person, not just with the person's academic achievements. (p. 27)

I have seen a great number of students in alternative programs who for extended periods of time appeared to be making little or no academic progress. Their teachers were frustrated and would complain that "nothing works." Over a period of time, however, most of these same students eventually became successful. It was only after their affective concerns were addressed and they came to trust their teachers and the rest of the staff that these students began to make academic progress. Affective components should be an integral part of the alternative program curriculum.

Alternative programs are often characterized by an innovative, experiential curriculum. With opportunities for community service, internships, externships, and school-to-work transition, students have the opportunity to earn academic credits for out-of-school learning experiences. At the same time, however, alternative programs need to emphasize basic skills instruction. It's important for those planning a new alternative program to avoid an either-or kind of thinking: that is, either an emphasis on innovation and experiential learning activities or an emphasis on basic skills instruction. Effective alternative programs can be *both* innovative and experiential and still emphasize basic skills such as reading, writing, and mathematics.

## 6. Separate Administrative Unit

Effective alternative programs generally have a separate administrative unit. The successful alternative program administrator must function as a leader in three areas: (a) management; (b) instruction; and (c) politics. Managerial and instructional leadership is required in order to establish the organizational flexibility that's necessary to respond to the unusual needs or circumstances of students who attend the alternative program. The administrator must work with students and teachers to create the sense of community that characterizes successful alternative programs.

Political leadership is needed in order to establish and maintain positive relations with the larger system(s) of which the alternative program is a part, as well as to ensure that the program is perceived as credible by outside organizations. Political leadership is also of importance when districts decide to form a consortium to establish an alternative program. Furthermore, because of the opposition that often results when an alternative program is located in a facility or on a site that is shared with a larger and more politically powerful organization (that may resent the presence of the alternative program), political skill is imperative on the part of the administrator. One of the principle reasons that many alternative programs are situated in less than desirable sites is a lack of political leadership at the district level.

## 7. Distinctive Mission and Family Atmosphere

Alternative schools have a clear mission, a sense of community and commitment, and shared values. Unlike large, traditional schools, which must be all things to all people, alternative schools can create specialized programs and utilize specialized teaching and counseling methodologies that have been targeted to clearly differentiated populations.

Characterized by a culture of concern and caring, alternative programs strive to develop a sense of "family" among all participants: students, teachers, counselors, support staff, and administrators. Cooperation is emphasized, rather than competition. Extremely positive relationships between students and teachers characterize alternative programs.

Mary E. Sweeney (1988) writes,

Alternative school programs assume in their philosophy that they are dealing with the "whole" of the child; including in their goal setting the physical, moral, social, emotional, spiritual, and aesthetic, as well as the intellectual developmental realms of a student. In true alternative schools, the assumption is made that different learners learn in distinct ways, thus the individual talents and needs of each child are what is valued. In the best interest of the learner, students and parents choose the type of program tailor made for individual student needs. (p. 22)

If you visit an effective alternative program and talk to students and teachers, you'll sense that relationships among students, faculty, staff, and administration are much closer and more informal than relationships in traditional schools. For example, it's not unusual for students in alternative programs to call their teachers by their first names.

I've always been amazed at the number of administrators and teachers who for some reason believe that requiring students to call you "mister" or "miss" indicates that they will respect you. At the alternative programs that I've administered, students didn't call me doctor or mister. They called me John. Two of the high schools where I've served as principal were countywide programs, where students with serious behavior disorders or emotional problems were admitted from many different high schools. At these different high schools, students previously had many different principals and assistant principals. Almost universally, the students called their former principals and assistant principals mister so-and-so—at least to their faces, they called them mister. In many instances, the students disliked or hated their former principals and assistant principals and called them every vile name imaginable when their backs were turned. If a kid's going to call me a bad name (and it's happened a lot), I'd much rather have him call me that name to my face. And no—I don't get angry when a kid calls me a name. That's his way of testing me.

Because I don't get angry with him, that same teenager is much more likely to come to me when he's in trouble and needs to talk. Difficult teenagers don't grant you real respect because you require them to call you mister, because you wear a suit, or because as an adult they automatically "owe" you their respect. It's not that easy. You have to earn their respect every day by how you live your life and how you relate to them and others. You can argue that kids should automatically grant this respect to their elders. By the same token, you could argue that the divorce rate shouldn't be so high, and that we shouldn't live in a world where AIDS and drive-by shootings can claim the lives of teenagers.

For those who believe that allowing teenagers to call adults by their first names is too permissive (and that you have to be either permissive or authoritative), I would argue that the practice is *neither* permissive *nor* authoritative. It simply makes you more accessible to students, who think it's neat that they can call their principal and teachers by their first names. The idea that you're either permissive or authoritarian, however, represents a false choice that many educators and parents believe to be true. I fully believe in holding teenagers accountable for their behavior. There are other ways, however, than acting in an authoritative manner to hold teenagers accountable and in the process foster greater self-reliance, more positive decision making, and increased self-control in them. These ways represent some of the most important affective goals that effective alternative programs achieve.


## 8. Flexible Teacher Roles and Program Autonomy

Because of the distinctive mission of alternative programs and the concept of school-as-family, teachers, counselors, and administrators who work in successful alternative programs accept a much broader and more flexible role than do teachers in traditional programs. Depending upon the need of the program, staff members may serve as counselors, attendance officers, bus drivers, and coaches.

Concerned not only with teaching English, science, math, and social studies, staff members in alternative schools encourage students to discuss their personal lives and problems.

As a principal of an alternative high school, my days may consist of writing curriculum, observing a teacher, counseling a student, planning new programs, writing a grant proposal, giving presentations, contacting parents, or attending meetings. I've cleaned up blood from fights and vomit from students who were drinking. I've also delivered eulogies for students who have died and once helped to deliver a baby. It's all part of a day's work.

Students and teachers in successful alternative programs share a sense of program ownership. Both students and teachers have considerable latitude in designing curricula, planning field trips, and determining credit arrangements. Encouraged to design and implement their own vision of education and schooling, students and teachers are freed from many of the standard rules and procedures that characterize traditional programs.

## 9. Access to Social Services

Because alternative programs often serve disruptive and disaffected students, arrangements should be made to provide students with access to social services on an as-needed basis. Ideally, these social services should be available to students on the school site. Services could include individual, group, and family counseling; access to basic health screening and counseling; employment services; probation; and welfare. Depending on the level of need, many social service providers may be willing to assign a caseworker to the alternative program one morning or afternoon a week.

## 10. Use of Technology

Because their need is greater, students who attend alternative programs should have at least the same level of access (or more access, if possible) to technology as do students who attend a traditional program. Unfortunately, because the majority of alternative programs are located in sites that tend to segregate or isolate students from the mainstream, access to state-of-the-art technology is often limited.

Hancock (1993) writes that,

For disadvantaged students, technological illiteracy implies constrained vocational opportunities; limited performance of basic living skills such as bill paying, grocery shopping, and banking. More than any other group, at-risk youngsters need the benefits and high support that carefully planned technology can provide them. When educators apply technology thoughtfully in their curricular programs, they affirm students' strengths. Technology offers students learning resources that complement and enhance their ability to learn. It helps students overcome economic disadvantage by accelerating performance outcomes as was never possible in the past. . . . Reports also show that for any student, use of technology is limited throughout the school day. Access to computers, for example, is often restricted to times when a teacher has scheduled a computer-related assignment for an entire class or has borrowed a computer for use in the classroom. Students are not often free to use a school's computer before or after school, and most disadvantaged students do not have access to computers at home. Moreover, few teachers require (or even recommend) that computers be used as tools to accomplish lesson-related tasks, nor do they make time to facilitate computer use. (p. 85)

Much has been written about the technological revolution and the "information superhighway." When they reach adulthood, it is the students who attend alternative programs who are most likely to be left off this information superhighway. The importance of technology in working with at-risk youth cannot be overemphasized.

All students—those attending both alternative and traditional schools—must become technologically literate in order to function successfully in today's and tomorrow's world.

## A Comment About Positive Synergies

*Synergy* is a term that comes from a discipline known as systems thinking. In simple terms, a positive synergistic response results when the interactions of separate individuals or units produce an overall effect that is greater than the sum of the individual parts. (A negative synergistic response results when the overall effect is less than the sum of the individual parts.)

In one of the most helpful books I've ever read in the field of management, *The Fifth Discipline* by Peter Senge (1990), he writes,

> Systems thinking is a discipline for seeing wholes. It is a framework for seeing interrelationships rather than things, for seeing patterns of change rather than static "snapshots." It is a set of general principles—distilled over the course of the twentieth century, spanning fields as diverse as the physical and social sciences, engineering, and management. It is also a set of specific tools and techniques, originating in two threads: in feedback concepts of cybernetics and in servo-mechanism engineering theory dating back to the nineteenth century. During the last thirty years, these tools have been applied to understand a wide range of corporate, urban, regional, political, and even physiological systems. And systems thinking is a sensibility—for the subtle interconnectedness that gives living systems their unique character. (p. 68)

I mention systems thinking and Senge's book at this point because if you succeed in setting up an effective alternative program— if you manage to incorporate most if not all of these 10 characteristics into your program—then you will also achieve a remarkable positive synergistic response. The "whole" of your new alternative program will be far greater than the sum of the individual parts. You need to develop a "systems mind-set."

## Conclusion

This chapter discussed the 10 key characteristics of alternative programs. Educators who are seeking to establish an effective alternative school should realize that excellence is difficult to achieve in any field. It is perhaps because excellence is difficult to achieve that the majority of alternative programs are alternative in name only. I urge those who seek to create an alternative program to create a program that exemplifies excellence and has a profound cognitive and affective effect upon students. Nothing less should be considered acceptable.

# 4

# Ten Alternative Models

Though there are thousands of alternative programs located across the United States, virtually all of these programs represent one of several basic alternative models (or prototypes) that will be discussed in this chapter. I've administered several of these models. In addition, I've visited many of the other models considered here. Before reviewing the advantages and disadvantages of each of these models, I'd like to restate three very important concepts from earlier chapters:

1. The richer or more desirable the site, the more powerful the effect of the site on modifying alternative school students' cognitive and affective states.
2. The richer or more desirable the site, the more likely the site will oppose the establishment of an alternative program on its premises.
3. The richer or more desirable the site, the more likely the culture of alternative school students will clash with the predominant culture of the host site.

It should be noted that many of the models discussed in this chapter are operating only at the secondary level. Innovative alternative models are very rarely found at the elementary school level. Though more prevalent at the middle school level, alternative programs are still the exception rather than the rule. In the discussion that follows, I'll treat elementary and middle school alternatives separately, as well as make suggestions as to the need for more innovative programs on the K-8 level.

Despite significant differences among many of these models, there are also numerous similarities concerning issues such as the importance of maintaining a positive relationship with the host site and the need to develop a sense of "family" within the alternative school. I'll make certain points that refer to all (or many) of these models only the first time the point needs to be discussed. Also, the alternative models that are discussed in this chapter have been listed in order of the degree of complexity involved in establishing each model. As a result, substantially more information is provided for the first three models.

1. College-Based Schools
2. Schools Without Walls
3. Mall-/Shopping District-Based Schools
4. Schools Organized Around a Single Unifying Theme and Located in an Environment Related to That Theme
5. Schools Organized Around a Single Unifying Theme But Located in an Environment Unrelated to That Theme
6. School Within a School (Full-Time Day Model)
7. School Within a School (After School Model)
8. Schools Located in an Isolated Location
9. Elementary School Model
10. Middle School Model

## 1. The College-Based Model

### The Advantages

Considering the three general principles listed in the beginning of this chapter, it's no wonder that what I believe to be the most powerful site—a college campus—is also the least prevalent model. You many recall from Chapter 3 that many researchers believe the social composition of the student body is the most powerful *school factor* (family background is of greater importance, however) that relates to student achievement. It is this concept that explains the success of the college-based model.

Many of the most successful alternative programs in the United States are located on college campuses. The idea behind college-based programs is as much sociological as pedagogical. The socialization effect that results from integrating disruptive and disaffected high school students into the adult environment of the college campus acts a "slingshot" for upward social mobility, with many students experiencing an educational and psychological catharsis. By altering the environment in which learning takes place, chronically disruptive and disaffected high school students, who carry college identification cards and participate in a full range of college activities, begin to think of themselves as college students. Once their mind-set has changed, profound cognitive and affective growth often follows.

## Middle College High School

One of the largest and best known alternative high schools is located on the campus of LaGuardia Community College, in the borough of Long Island, New York City. Middle College High School, as the program is known, has achieved great success in helping disruptive and disaffected students to turn their lives around. Middle College High School's low dropout rate (15% compared to a citywide average of 46%) and high college acceptance rate (85%) testify to the effectiveness of the program. Middle College High School's more than 500 students are accepted from all areas of Queens. The high school students have access to the college facilities, with most taking some college courses by the time they are seniors.

Middle College High School has won recognition as one of the top public high schools in the country. In fact, the Presidential-appointed Carnegie Commission, in its comprehensive study on secondary education that reported in such detail what was wrong with American public education, singled out Middle College High School for special praise, calling it one of the few high schools that was doing things right.

Writing about Middle College High School, Lieberman (1985) explains that,

> The power of the site is another clue toward understanding these attitudes. Holding high school classes in a college

setting reinforces the concept of freedom. It provides an atmosphere where secondary students subtly modify their behavior. The college environment not only penetrates the insularity of the teenage culture but also encourages the adolescents to take advantage of the prerogatives of adult status. They commingle with college students, and they respond maturely. The peer model of the college student enables them to perceive themselves two years later. They recognize that they too can succeed. The feedback in motivation is obvious. Middle College students sport a college ID; they use the bookstore; they work out in the gym. (p. 13)

### Atlantic County Alternative High School

As I mentioned in Chapter 2, I set up and administered a countywide college-based program for chronically disruptive and disaffected students. I've also served as a consultant to several districts or consortiums of districts that have set up college-based programs.

The college-based program that I established, the Atlantic County Alternative High School (ACAHS), is located on the campus of Atlantic Community College in Mays Landing, New Jersey (about 20 miles east of Atlantic City). Many of the students who attend ACAHS have already dropped out of school, are on the verge of dropping out of school, or have been excluded from a traditional public high school as a consequence of having committed acts of serious disruptive behavior, including weapons offenses. Some of these adolescents have been previously incarcerated. The majority of these students, all of whom are either chronically disruptive or chronically disaffected, come from families that would be characterized as from a lower socioeconomic background. Table 4.1 summarizes the typical problems presented by students in their home schools prior to acceptance at ACAHS.

ACAHS, which boasts an 86% graduation rate since its inception in 1986, has received awards for excellence from the New Jersey State School Board, the New Jersey Department of Education, the New Jersey Alternative Education Association, *USA Today*, and the Association for Children of New Jersey. The program *completely immerses* chronically disruptive and disaffected high school students into the college mainstream. Many of the graduates of ACAHS (the majority of whose parents did not complete high school) go on to college, thus

**Table 4.1** Problems Created/Experienced by ACAHS Students Prior to Acceptance to Alternative Program

| Problem | Percentage of Student Body Involved |
|---|---|
| Acts of Violence (in school) | 20 |
| Acts of Violence (out of school) | 40 |
| Basic Academic Skills Deficiencies | 50 |
| Chronic Class Cutting | 60 |
| Chronic School Discipline Problems | 75 |
| Dysfunctional Home Situation | 60 |
| Probation | 33 |
| Suicide Attempts | 10 |
| Unusual Living Arrangements | 60 |
| Substance Abuse | 40 |
| Single Parent | 20 |

validating the concept that college-based programs provide unprecedented opportunities for upward social mobility. Atlantic Community College provides ACAHS students with full-time use of classrooms inside college buildings.

ACAHS students are taught by fully certified high school teachers, employees of the Atlantic County Vocational Technical School District. In addition, academically qualified students are permitted to enroll in college classes on a tuition-free, space-available basis. On the final day of registration, if seats are open in a college class, alternative high school students are permitted to register for free college classes. A student who passes a college course can earn high school credits on the basis of proficiency for successfully completing the college course. The student also "banks" those college credits for use subsequent to graduation from high school.

ACAHS has full use of all college facilities, including the gymnasium, library, computer and science laboratories, student life center, and theater. Students participate in many college clubs and activities, such as the minority student union, campus newspaper, and radio station. Internships are available in many campus departments.

What makes college-based alternative programs so effective? Assuming that these programs can incorporate all the components that make any alternative program successful, the critical variable that differentiates this model from others is the power of the site in modifying student behavior. In Atlantic County, for example, I compiled 9 years of data related to discipline referrals for alternative high school students when the college was in session and compared these figures with the number of referrals when the college was out of session. In order to understand these data, you must realize that the alternative high school is in session for 180 days. The college, however, is in session for approximately 140 days (28 weeks). Thus, there are approximately 40 days when the high school is in session, but the college is not holding classes. (This period includes the long break between the fall and spring semesters, the college spring break, and about 2 weeks in June.) During these 40 days, the ACAHS students are virtually the only students on campus, and the sociology of the site—the critical variable in modifying the behavior of the high school students—is dramatically altered. Over a 9-year period, 60% of all discipline referrals occurred during those 40-day periods each year when the high school was in session, but the college was not in session. Thus, rather than discipline problems being randomly distributed throughout the 180-day school year, 60% of all discipline problems took place during a period that represented only 22% of the school year.

## *The College-Based Model: The Disadvantages*

It can be extremely difficult to establish a college-based alternative program for at-risk students. Political opposition to such programs is both substantial and understandable. Few colleges are willing to open their campus to disruptive students and the accompanying problems that these students bring with them and create on campus.

Lieberman (1985) writes,

> The institution sponsoring partnership must have cooperation at the highest level of administration from both the high school and the college sector—superintendent to chancellor. Programs which begin counselor-to-counselor or faculty-to-faculty have trouble making it. Similarly, the community and the educators need time to understand the new structure and to accept its non-traditional approach. Although cooperation at the top is necessary, some projects fail because they have not included all participants in the planning. High school personnel need full partnership in every project design. (p. 21)

Establishing this high level of partnership between the district and college can be most difficult. Also, those who administer college-based programs should be aware of certain patterns that tend to develop over a period of several years. The deeper the integration of chronically disruptive students into the college environment, the faster and more powerful the modification of their behavior. In Atlantic County, for the average student the change process—defined as the amount of time it takes for the student to overcome the cognitive and affective problems that prevented her or him from experiencing success in the traditional school environment—takes about 18 months. As part of this integration process, a certain amount of disruption (fights, substance abuse, vandalism, thefts, and inappropriate language) that adversely impacts the college is inevitable.

## Recoil Effect

Because of these acts of disruption, a recoil effect usually occurs. At this point, colleges tend to reevaluate their commitment to such programs. Alternative high school students may be stereotyped as "delinquents, thugs, and hooligans." The entire group tends to be blamed for the misbehavior of one student. For example, one of my students at ACAHS once took a mouse from a college science lab and "nuked" it in a microwave oven in a crowded college lounge. For several months, college personnel talked about the incident. Because of the infamous "mouse in the microwave," as well as other incidents of misbehavior and vandalism, college employees began to ask, "Why are these people here?" College students complained, "I pay tuition. Why do I have to put up with this kind of behavior?"

College-based programs that survive the initial few years must develop methods to reduce the extent of this disruption and to publicize the success of the majority of participants, thereby minimizing the recoil effect.

## Population Softens

Another result of the recoil effect is a tendency for the alternative high school population to "soften" over the years. In some instances, college-based programs that were initially established to deal with the most hardcore cases wind up excluding all but passive, disaffected students. Though these programs still perform a value to society, such programs are affecting dropout rates, as opposed to diverting seriously at-risk adolescents from the juvenile justice system (the intent of several college-based programs with which I am familiar).

In Atlantic County, we have made a concerted effort to resist softening the population and continue to serve some of the more hardcore cases, including students who previously have been incarcerated and who have committed acts of violence. The college is involved in selecting students and has veto power as to which students are accepted into the alternative high school. Atlantic Community College believes that is has an obligation to serve the entire community and has been willing to give more difficult students a second chance.

## Continuous Tension

Although alternative programs are characterized by more informal and closer relationships between students, staff, and administration, at the same time effective college-based alternative programs involve continuous tension between the high school staff and high school administration and between the high school and college. This tension is a necessary by-product of the change process that occurs when working with a chronically disruptive population. Simply put, the entire high school staff—faculty as well as administration—must accept substantially more negative student behavior than would be tolerated in a traditional school. This does not mean that students are not held accountable for their behavior. To dismiss students with a history of fighting after their first fight in the alternative high school, however, would be unconscionable and create a counterproductive "revolving door" situation. Teachers will sometimes complain that they want a student permanently removed from their classroom after a serious negative incident. Though I may make some kind of temporary arrangements to accommodate a teacher, seldom will I permanently remove a student, and this creates a level of tension.

Similarly, the college must be willing to accept some degree of inconvenience when it agrees to host such programs. Unless there is a degree of *manageable tension* between the high school and college, it's generally indicative that the program has abandoned its original mission to serve chronically disruptive students. If there are few or no complaints from the college about the program, then the students may not really be disruptive.

*Public Relations and Security*

I spend about half of my time on issues related to school public relations and security. I patrol campus a minimum of 2 hours a day and carry a walkie-talkie, with which I communicate with teachers and college security. The importance of public relations and security in such college-based programs cannot be overemphasized. When people ask me what I do every day, I reply that I manage the *cultural clash* that results from the integration of chronically disruptive high school students into the college community. Managed effectively, this cultural clash can be minimized, but it can never be eliminated.

## 2. Schools Without Walls

### The Advantages

The schools-without-walls model is the most intriguing prototype on this list. Similar to the term *open classrooms,* the phrase *schools without walls* invokes permissive images of the 1960s when—according to many—American education lost its direction and academic standards were seriously compromised. I agree that the 1960s and 1970s represent a confusing period for American education. To blame open classrooms or schools without walls is patently unfair, however. Managed effectively, they represent excellent educational concepts. Managed ineffectively, they can prove disastrous.

The schools-without-walls model is built upon the premise that the entire community can be a classroom. Such a program as Philadelphia's well-known Parkway School utilizes locations such as businesses, hospitals, museums, zoos, courtrooms, airports, aquariums, theaters, and government offices as learning centers. In a very real sense, this model can be considered a kind of traveling magnet school, with the curriculum developed to match the opportunities and experiences available for students at each site. Most such programs operate from a base, or home site classroom or school. Schools without walls can prove extremely effective in providing students with hands-on learning experiences and exposure to real-world activities—something from which all students, whether at risk or not, can benefit. In addition, students come into close contact with the staff of each site, thereby fostering positive relationships with large numbers of responsible and significant adults that can last for years.

A student attending a school without walls might spend a 4-week "rotation" at a hospital, then go on to another 4-week rotation at a business, zoo, museum, and so forth. Because of the positive experiences they have at these sites, many students decide to seek additional training in a field related to the site. A student who enjoys a rotation at a hospital site may choose to study nursing in college. A student who finds the business world suited to her interests may choose a college major in accounting, finance, economics, or management.

## Schools Without Walls: The Disadvantages

Transportation is a major issue in developing a schools-without-walls program. Because both public transportation and educational and cultural opportunities are much more available in big cities, schools without walls tend to be located in places such as Philadelphia, New York, and Chicago. If your district is located in a rural or suburban area, this model will be extremely difficult (perhaps impossible) to implement and may not be cost-effective. Another potential problem involves program size and the availability of space at each site. Larger programs will either need a significant amount of space at each site or will be required to operate multiple rotations at multiple sites, which may further increase the cost of transportation. Cost is also an issue in regard to the use of community-based sites. Because at least 75% of most school budgets is composed of personnel costs, there may be only limited funds available for rental of space in community facilities. If the site will provide your program access to facilities without cost—or for a minimal cost—then cost may not be a prohibitive factor. (Remember that the schools-without-walls program will also incur costs related to the maintenance of a home base, either a classroom, classrooms, or an entire school building.)

The planning and coordination required to effectively organize a school without walls can prove enormous. A specific site-based curriculum should be developed for each location. To insure continuity in the curriculum, at a minimum students should have the opportunity to "do" English, math, science, and social studies at each site. You should avoid offering only science at a hospital site or only social studies at a museum site.

As is the case with the college-based model, relations between the alternative school and the host site(s) are of great importance. Many of the more desirable sites—a museum, for example—may be adverse to permitting disruptive secondary students to utilize their facility. Furthermore, positive relations must be established between the school without walls and *each site* that the school wishes to utilize. This, too, can be difficult because of the necessity of dealing with numerous organizations, personalities, and expectations. One site may have far different expectations concerning student comportment than another.

A school without walls should ideally hold classes at community-based sites for most or all of the academic year. Because of the kinds of problems already mentioned, however, it is not unusual for students who attend schools without walls to actually wind up spending more days attending classes *within* walls (at the home site classroom or school) than at community-based sites. Thus, these schools must develop an entirely separate alternative program that will operate within the walls of a traditional classroom or school.

In conclusion, schools without walls—though difficult to establish and maintain—can represent outstanding educational programs. Whether the positive outcomes that can result from such programs justify the substantial commitment of personnel and resources that are necessary in order to establish a schools-without-walls model should be considered before a district establishes this model.

## 3. Mall-/Shopping District-Based School

### The Advantages

From my experience, it is easier to establish a program inside a mall or a shopping district than it is to set up a college-based school or a school without walls. The district usually must deal directly with only one organization, either the corporation that manages the mall, the local municipal government, or a local business consortium, which in turn represents the interests of the establishments that will be impacted by the alternative school. Once the alternative school is established, however, staff and students must make every effort to develop positive relations with all their neighbors. The most common arrangement is for the mall or shopping district either to donate or to lease (usually for a cost below the actual market value that would normally be charged for use of the facility) classroom and office space to the alternative school.

## Combining School and Work

Research has shown that one of the most common reasons given by students for dropping out of school is a desire or necessity to work. Mall- and shopping district-based schools provide at-risk students with substantial opportunities to attend school as well as to work. Because students can walk from school to work, transportation is not a problem. Students have opportunities for ongoing positive interactions with a large number of adults who are not members of the alternative school staff. Because of these interactions between students and other adults, it is relatively easy to establish adopt-a-school and mentor programs.

Another essential component of the mall or shopping district school curriculum should be a school-to-work transition program. Hudelson (1994) writes that,

> The lack of a comprehensive and effective school-to-work transition system also has had a significant impact on students. In the 1980's, the gap in earnings between high school graduates and college graduates doubled; for those without high school degrees, the gap grew even wider. Not only has the lack of school-to-work assistance had a negative impact on the earnings potential of our young people, but it also has cost American businesses plenty. This affects our entire economy.... The work-based learning component must include a planned program of job training and work experiences, at least some of which must be paid; workplace mentoring; instruction in general workplace competencies; and broad instruction related to industry. The school-based learning component must include:
>
> - career awareness and career exploration and counseling;
> - a requirement that interested students select a career major no later than the start of the 11th grade;
> - a program of study designed to meet state-established academic content standards;

- a program of instruction and curriculum that integrates academic and vocational learning and incorporates instruction in a variety of elements of an industry;
- regularly scheduled evaluations of and ongoing consultation with students and school dropouts to identify their academic strengths and weaknesses, academic progress, workplace knowledge, goals and the need for additional learning opportunities to master core academic and vocational skills;
- mechanisms that enable students participating in a school-to-work program to transfer to a postsecondary program. (p. 17)

### Delivery of On-Site Government, Social, and Health Services

Mall- and shopping district-based schools are also excellent locations for the delivery of on-site government and social services, as well as an initial level of health care screening for students. Many at-risk students are involved with one or more government agencies or social service providers, such as welfare, probation, counseling, or employability training. Depending upon the extent of the need, these agencies and social service and health care providers are often willing to operate a satellite office in the mall or shopping district. (Personnel who staff these satellite offices also will provide services to the general public.) If the need does not justify the establishment of a satellite office, government agencies and social service and health care providers may be willing to assign personnel for 1 day a week to the alternative school. If these kinds of services can be provided on the school site, students won't have to miss significant amounts of class time in order to travel to keep appointments with welfare case workers or probation officers. In addition, this arrangement also facilitates the sharing of information. Teachers can speak directly to case workers or probation officers, thereby coordinating the delivery of educational and social services.

Another advantage of this model is that students generally like to be at malls, which usually offer a variety of inexpensive fast food restaurants, convenient shopping, movies, health clubs, and recreational facilities such as arcades and pool tables. Arrangements can be made so that students can utilize all these facilities.

*Advantages to the Mall or Shopping District*

There are also advantages to the mall or shopping district. If classroom space is donated or leased to the alternative school at a cost less than the actual market value, the mall or shopping district may claim a tax deduction. In providing classroom and office space to the alternative school, the mall or shopping district may also appear to be a "good neighbor" in the community, thereby improving public relations. Furthermore, students who attend the school will patronize many of the mall or shopping district's stores, which will also benefit by having a convenient pool of teenage labor.

## Mall-/Shopping District-Based School: The Disadvantages

Assuming that the mall or shopping district is willing to provide the alternative school with sufficient space at a reasonable cost, there are only three issues that must be addressed under this heading. First, I have some concerns about the culture of the mall or shopping district and the socialization effect that tends to occur when adolescents spend an inordinate time in or around commercial establishments.

To illustrate my point, allow me a slight digression. Every school has a predominant culture. It's something that an experienced observer can sense literally within a few minutes of walking into the building. I remember visiting an alternative "school" for adjudicated adolescents in Florida. Before I entered the facility, I was warned that these were some of the toughest teenagers in the state. I was also told that many of the teenagers had to be kept behind bars because they frequently fought or were potentially dangerous to staff members. The great majority of the staff was male. Several of the staff members were the size of pro football linemen. As I toured the program, I was appalled by the utter joylessness that pervaded the school. Students appeared sullen and depressed. Some look frightened. There was none of the sense of family that characterizes effective alternative programs. Nevertheless, the staff prided themselves on the level of "control" that they exercised over their students and their ability to instill harsh discipline. It was obvious that size and physical strength were considered important in the culture of this program, which was really a prison masquerading as an alternative school. Within such a culture, it was no wonder that students were joyless and frequently fought. Regardless of the level of delinquent behavior in their backgrounds, it was apparent that these adolescents were being negatively socialized by the culture of this facility.

So, too, adolescents can be powerfully influenced by the commercial culture (and the concomitant values associated with that culture) of the mall or shopping district. Schools—whether alternative or traditional—located in noncommercial facilities do not have to contend with the commercial culture that pervades malls and shopping districts.

In addition, there is the possibility that students may be exploited by employers. School-to-work transitions programs are designed to provide students with opportunities for *meaningful* postsecondary employment. With a need for cheap labor, employers in malls and shopping districts may seek to place students in minimum wage jobs that offer no benefits and little opportunity for advancement. The school's work coordinator should be careful that such exploitation is not allowed to occur.

The two disadvantages mentioned in the preceding paragraphs represent problems that the location may create for students who attend the alternative school. The third disadvantage—issues such as loitering, shoplifting, harassing customers—represent problems that *students* may create for the mall or shopping district. Strategies similar to those discussed under the college-based model should be used to promote positive relations between the alternative school and the host site.

## 4. Schools Organized Around a Single Unifying Theme and Located in an Environment Related to That Theme

### The Advantages

This model is more commonly referred to as a magnet school. The idea for organizing a school around a single unifying theme provides students with opportunities for *intensive exploration* of that theme. The location, such as a museum, theater, art gallery, or medical or high-tech center, provides students with real-world experiences as they consistently "do" a subject. Many of the students who attend these schools are gifted in one or several areas.

Schlemmer (1981) writes about a Grand Rapids, Michigan, school located adjacent to a city zoo.

> The program focuses on environmental education and global education, the latter stressed through daily study of current events. The program has been structured to fit its setting; thus students make extensive use of the zoo and its surrounding park area. But the model is adaptable to any site, including a regular classroom, and to any program focus. A program with the same mission, concentrating on history, might be housed in a museum, for instance; one focusing on research might be situated in a library. (p. 558)

One of the real strengths of magnet schools involves the program's ability to respond to diverse learning styles.

Doyle and Levine (1984) write,

> Magnet schools also afford choices to youngsters who have differing learning styles and differing interests. Magnet schools that focus on music and art, on vocational education, on the humanities, on science and mathematics, or on any of a number of other areas make good sense, both pedagogically and socially. Moreover, magnet schools have an ambience that has a positive effect on personal behavior. Thus magnet schools can set standards of dress and behavior that would be impossible to enforce in comprehensive high schools. For example, a magnet school could easily require community service as a condition of graduation, whereas such a requirement would be intrusive and onerous if it were expected of all students in a given school district. (p. 267)

Though not necessarily located in an environment intrinsically related to the program, several of the best known magnet schools are among the elite schools in the United States. These schools include the Boston Latin School, which was established in 1635; Philadelphia's Central High School; Chicago's Lane Tech; Manhattan's New York High School of the Performing Arts; San Francisco's Lowell High School; Queen's Aviation High School; and the Bronx High School of Science.

Not all magnet schools are for gifted students. For example, there are numerous programs in industrial locations that are organized around vocational-high-tech themes. I've found that these vocational-high-tech centers respond to the learning style of many at-risk students, who desire "hands-on" educational experiences.

### School Organized Around a Single Unifying Theme and Located in an Environment Related to That Theme: The Disadvantages

There are two distinct disadvantages related to this model. First, many magnet schools tend to be elitist and often have rigorous entrance requirements that may prevent seriously at-risk students from gaining acceptance. At-risk students who are accepted may have difficulties conforming to the academic and social expectations of the magnet school. Second, there are a limited number of sites that are willing to serve as hosts for magnet schools. Those sites that are willing to accept such programs rarely provide more than a few classrooms or offices for the schools' use. Thus, the number of site-specific schools is small, and the enrollment in such schools is limited.

## 5. Schools Organized Around a Single Unifying Theme But Located in an Environment Unrelated to That Theme

### The Advantages and Disadvantages

*Because* the number of site-specific schools is small and the enrollment is limited, many magnet schools are located on sites that are not specifically related to the theme of the school. The same advantages that I listed under site-specific magnet schools apply in this section. The only difference between the two models is that site-specific locations can provide more hands-on kinds of learning activities for students.

The disadvantages are the same as those listed for site-specific schools.

## 6. School-Within-a-School (Full-Time Day Model)

### *The Advantages*

Because this model is so easy to establish, the school-within-a-school is the most common full-time day alternative model. Because the alternative program is usually located in a wing of a district school, it requires virtually no political effort to establish. There are few additional costs, other than those involving the staffing of the alternative program. Students attending the alternative school have access to all the same facilities as students who attend the traditional program in the same building. Nor do special arrangements have to be made for transportation.

This model also facilitates the return of alternative students to the mainstream, should that be the goal of the program or the desire of the students. (Remember from a previous chapter, however, that in the most effective alternative schools students generally remain in the alternative programs until graduation.)

Based on the assumption that most readers of *How to Establish an Alternative School* already are quite familiar with the organization and culture of traditional schools, little more needs to be said here. Simply imagine two schools with two distinct cultures operating within the same building.

### *School-Within-a-School (Full-Time Day Model): The Disadvantages*

The last sentence of the preceding paragraph highlights the one serious problem with this model. Do you have one set of rules for students who attend the traditional school and a different set of rules for students who attend the alternative school in a different section of the same building? Can there be two sets of rules within the same building?

From my experience with this model, you *must* have two set of rules and policies if the alternative program is to prove successful. At-risk students find it difficult to adhere to the same rules and policies as other students. In fact, it is precisely *because* they find it difficult to follow the same rules and policies that alternative schools were established in the first place. As a result of the coexistence of two sets of rules, a degree of tension will arise between administration and staff of the traditional program and their counterparts in the alternative school. For example, let's consider the attendance policy. A student in a traditional school may be permitted 14 unexcused absences before she or he loses credit. In the alternative school, at-risk students—because of the severity of their problems—might be permitted three or four times that many absences without losing credit. Invariably, students (and their parents) who lose credit after 14 absences in the traditional school will complain that they are being treated unfairly compared with students in the alternative school.

I could list many examples of the tension that arises when two sets of rules operate within the same building. If a student is sent from the traditional school to the alternative school because of a history of fighting, where do you send that student after his first fight in the alternative school? What if the fight occurred between a student in the alternative school and a student in the traditional school? Who administers the discipline . . . the principal of the traditional school, the principal of the alternative school, or both? Also, students in the alternative school will generally develop a positive relationship with their teachers in the program. They often have very negative feelings, however, about administrators and teachers in the traditional school. What happens when an alternative school student disobeys an administrator or teacher from the traditional school? What about students calling their teachers by their first names? How about more significant issues, such as the awarding of credits in nontraditional ways?

As is the case with the college-based model, a certain degree of *manageable tension* is to be expected between traditional and alternative schools that operate within the same building. Structures must be put in place that will alleviate the severity of this tension. Discipline decisions should be made cooperatively by the administrators of the traditional and alternative schools.

For those who would argue that it's impossible to have two sets of rules operating within the same building, I would suggest that for the most serious issues (substance abuse, weapons offenses, etc.) both schools should operate under the same set of rules. For less serious disciplinary infractions and for other policies such as discipline and credit awarding, two sets of rules are needed if the alternative program is to prove successful. If you're unwilling to accept this idea, you probably don't want to establish an alternative program in the same building as a traditional school.

One final point needs to be made. Over time, powerful organizational forces (such as the tension that originates from the existence of two sets of rules) tend to "dilute" the culture of the alternative program when it is located within the same building as a traditional school. I am familiar with several in-house alternative schools that have existed for more than 10 years. These schools, which started out with the hope of "breaking the mold" and with markedly divergent views about education and the learning process, today seem little more than mini-traditional schools distinguished from the mainstream only by more informal relationships between students and teachers.

## 7. Schools-Within-a-School (After School Model)

### *The Advantages*

The After School Model is very common. To a large extent, it exists because administrators and faculty in traditional schools are unwilling to accept the tension that results from having two sets of rules existing within the same building. The advantages of this model are similar to the advantages of the full-time in-house alternative model. The most significant difference is that the alternative program does not have to concern itself with the traditional school and its blanket set of rules and policies.

### *Schools-Within-a-School (After School Model): The Disadvantages*

In theory, the school-within-a-school after school program does not *have* to be inferior to other models. I have visited many of these programs, however, and most of them seem little more than after school detention halls, staffed by part-time teachers who have no significant involvement with the students other than to take attendance and hand out worksheets. The problem with this model reflects precisely the reason that it was created in the first place—to isolate, segregate, and exclude at-risk students from the mainstream. As is frequently the case with these programs, student are sent to the after school program for a predetermined period of time after accumulating a certain number of demerits, referrals, or suspensions.

During their stay at the alternative school, students have the opportunity to "work off" their demerits by demonstrating good attendance and behavior and the ability to stay on task in their classes. After they have worked off enough demerits, they "earn" the right to return to the traditional program (where they were unsuccessful to begin with).

This sounds like a soft prison to me. An after school alternative program may be better than no program at all. And not all after school programs are ineffective. For the most part, though, this is a punitive model and should be avoided.

## 8. Schools Located in an Isolated Location

### The Advantages

As the name suggests, the "advantage" of schools located in isolated places is their isolation. Whatever happens at the isolated location alternative school involves only the students and staff of the program. The only advantage of this model that I can think of is that (if you chose to) you can hold on to students who commit particularly egregious offenses within your building. You don't have to worry what the administrator of the traditional school will think, what the college faculty will say, or what the patrons of the mall, zoo, aquarium, or museum will say.

### Schools Located in an Isolated Location:
### The Disadvantages

In general, schools in isolated locations tend to have punitive programs that isolate, segregate, and exclude students from the mainstream. I had one memorable experience administering this model. In the early 1980s, I received a call from the head of the Special Education Department of a local college. The professor explained that a school with which he was connected needed an interim principal. The regular principal had been injured in a motorcycle accident. The professor told me that the students were a rough group who "fought a lot." The program, a countywide school for emotionally disturbed adolescents, was located inside an old church building in a rural area.

I took the assignment. On the morning of my first day, a large male student was giving a female teacher a hard time in the corridor. I intervened and spoke with the student, trying to calm him down. After a few minutes, the student calmed down enough to return to class. Afterwards, the teacher confronted me on how I had dealt with the incident. I'll never forget her saying, "You're a big guy. Why didn't you just hit him?" As was the case with the prison-like school in Florida, the isolated location of this school contributed to the development of a school culture for both staff and students that was characterized by violence.

Aside from the fact that these models are often punitive, transportation and costs can also be prohibitive factors with the isolated location alternative school.

## 9. Elementary School Model

The need for early identification in elementary school is critical. Van Ruiten (1990) writes that,

Although the idea of providing assistance to at-risk students at as early an age as possible seems to be just common sense, it is only in the past decade that early intervention programs have been developed and become widespread. More and more educators and mental health professionals are realizing that the earlier the intervention, the greater the chance of producing meaningful change in a child. Results from programs that intervene when students are already in trouble behaviorally or academically are often disappointing because by the time a student is in trouble, the behaviors and attitudes are deeply ingrained. (p. 20)

Many researchers have demonstrated that the problems that afflict students in the primary grades are accurate predictors of problems that will affect them as adolescents. For example, Hunter and Kellam (1990) report that,

Low achievement in first grade is related to depression in adolescence, while disobeying rules or habitually fighting predict later risk of dependency, drug use, and dropping out. Shy children who sit alone, have no friends, and do not participate in class often have anxiety problems as teenagers. (p. 17)

### Predicting Students Who May Be At Risk

Early intervention with at-risk students can mean the difference between a successful student and a dropout. Successful early intervention requires two components: accurate identification and appropriate intervention.

### Profile of an At-Risk Student

Teacher judgment is important in determining the identity of those children who may be at risk; however, this determination is often significantly affected by the composition of the class in which a student is functioning. The social, emotional, and academic norms of the class significantly influence teachers' perceptions. Therefore, more objective data should be included in measurements of risk.

Hundreds of studies have provided an accurate picture of elementary school students who are most likely to be at risk.

General characteristics of such students include

Low family socioeconomic level

Poor sense of self-esteem

Inadequate goals and lack of future orientation

Student apathetic or withdrawn

Student angry, defiant, or overly disruptive

Single parent or broken family structure

Low standardized test scores

Low aspirations and parents with low expectations

### The Phi Delta Kappa Study of At-Risk Children

Phi Delta Kappa conducted an extensive study of who is at risk and ranked 45 weighted variables to help to identify such students. The Phi Delta Kappa study includes items more applicable to middle school and high school students (see Table 4.2).

**Table 4.2** The Phi Delta Kappa Study of At-Risk Children

| Number/Item | Value/Weight |
|---|---|
| 1. Attempted suicide during the past year | 465.4 |
| 2. Used drugs or engaged in substance abuse | 465.0 |
| 3. Has been a drug "pusher" during the past year | 462.1 |
| 4. Student's sense of self-esteem is negative | 455.4 |
| 5. Was involved in pregnancy during past year | 450.6 |
| 6. Was expelled from school during the past year | 443.3 |
| 7. Consumes alcohol regularly | 441.0 |
| 8. Was arrested for illegal activity | 438.1 |
| 9. Parents have negative attitudes toward education | 437.1 |
| 10. Has several brothers or sisters who dropped out | 432.1 |
| 11. Was sexually or physically abused last year | 431.9 |
| 12. Failed two courses last school year | 429.2 |
| 13. Was suspended from school twice last year | 429.2 |
| 14. Student was absent more than 20 days last year | 429.2 |
| 15. Parent drinks excessively and is an alcoholic | 411.6 |
| 16. Was retained in grade [i.e., "Held Back"] | 403.1 |
| 17. One parent attempted suicide last year | 399.7 |
| 18. Scored below 20th percentile on standardized test | 397.0 |
| 19. Other family members used drugs during past year | 389.0 |
| 20. Attended three or more schools during past 5 years | 383.2 |
| 21. Average grades were below "C" last school year | 380.3 |
| 22. Was arrested for driving while intoxicated | 364.9 |
| 23. Has an IQ below 90 | 353.7 |
| 24. Parents divorced or separated last year | 353.6 |
| 25. Father is unskilled during the past year | 346.3 |
| 26. Father or mother died during the past year | 345.4 |
| 27. Diagnosed as being in Special Education | 336.2 |
| 28. English is not language used most often in home | 335.5 |
| 29. Mother is unskilled laborer who is unemployed | 329.7 |
| 30. Lives in inner-city, urban area | 321.7 |
| 31. The mother is only parent living in the home | 320.3 |
| 32. Is year older than other students in same grade | 319.5 |
| 33. Mother did not graduate from high school | 315.9 |
| 34. Father lost his job during the past year | 305.8 |
| 35. Was dropped from athletic teams during the past year | 296.2 |
| 36. Experienced a serious illness or accident | 295.1 |
| 37. Does not participate in extracurricular activities | 295.0 |
| 38. Parent had major change in health status | 294.9 |
| 39. Had a close friend die during past year | 293.7 |
| 40. Had a brother or sister die during the past year | 288.8 |
| 41. Father did not graduate from high school | 263.0 |
| 42. Changed schools during the year | 262.6 |
| 43. Changed place or residence during the past year | 253.3 |
| 44. Has three or more brothers or sisters | 175.3 |
| 45. Is the youngest child in the family | 157.7 |

*Effective Intervention Strategies and Programs*

Once at-risk students have been identified, intervention strategies and programs should be developed. Effective intervention strategies will

1. Include comprehensive approaches that focus on as many at-risk conditions as possible
2. Stress the importance of self-concept and its connection with achievement and aspirations
3. Help students develop the social skills that are required for successful interactions with other children and adults
4. Empower both teachers and students to agree cooperatively upon the methods and materials to be used in the classroom
5. Include parents and the community in the selection/implementation of appropriate intervention activities
6. Integrally involve students in their education, thereby strengthening the connection between motivation and success and helping the learner assume greater responsibility for her or his own progress
7. Establish high expectations for at-risk students, with an emphasis on acceleration rather than remediation or retention
8. Benefit from strong leadership and administrative support at the building and district level and include a long-term intervention model

Once the predictors are selected and at-risk students have been identified, an action plan can be developed to address the problem.

*Three Intervention Programs at the Elementary School Level*

Many programs are being used in elementary schools in order to intervene with students who have been identified as potentially at risk. Three programs that have been proven successful in accelerating the progress of low-achieving children are discussed in this section.

*1. Reading Recovery.* This program is designed to accelerate the literacy development of children who are having difficulty learning to read. Students in first-grade classes participate in an intensive daily 30-minute tutorial. As part of this tutorial, students develop self-monitoring strategies. Within 12 to 14 weeks, the average Reading Recovery student has made sufficient progress to be discontinued from the tutorial. The majority of children who participate in the program progress satisfactorily without further assistance. For information write: Dr. Carol Lyons, Ohio Reading Recovery, Ohio State University, 200 Ramseyer Hall, Columbus, OH 43210.

2. *Success for All.* This program operates on the K-3 level and includes an all-day kindergarten. Rather than age grouping, students are regrouped by reading level and experience a core reading and language arts curriculum. School personnel are also reorganized to allow for special reading tutors to work with individual children experiencing difficulty. Cooperative learning is emphasized, as well as at-home reading every night. Family support teams that include teachers, social workers, and parent liaisons help to facilitate closer cooperation between home and school. For information write: Dr. Robert Slavin, Center for Research on Effective Schooling for Disadvantaged Students, Johns Hopkins University, 3305 N. Charles Street, Baltimore, MD 21218.

3. *Accelerated Schools.* These projects empower faculty and staff by involving them in curriculum and instructional decisions. A 6-year effort, AS projects systematically restructure elementary schools so that all children—including those most at risk—can learn. For information write: Dr. Henry Levin, Accelerated Schools Project, 402 South CERAS, Stanford University, Stanford CA 94305-3084.

### Additional Suggestions: Elementary School Intervention

There is substantial evidence that the implementation of full day kindergarten and the reduction of student-staff ratios in the elementary grades can produce lasting cognitive and affective growth. The use of technology throughout the curriculum is also important, as is the availability of support services such as those provided by speech therapists, psychologists, and social workers. Flexible promotion standards should be initiated, so that children are not locked into meeting rigid and frequently unrealistic requirements in order to progress to the next grade. The importance of a comprehensive and long-term intervention approach is critical.

There are thousands of such early intervention programs operating in our nation's elementary schools. Almost all of them provide extra assistance to students believed to be potentially at risk. Can these kinds of limited assistance programs do enough, however? Do we need full-scale alternative schools at this level?

Sweeney and Wheelock (1989) report that,

> Research findings concerning characteristics of successful programs highlighted by the Project of Alternatives in Education (PAE) and the NCEES team also dovetail with those of researcher Eileen Foley (1983) and others at the Public Education Association of New York. In in-depth studies of alternative schools in New York City, PAE identified certain program elements which characterize effective alternative programs, concluding that alternative programs can help unsuccessful students complete their high school education. However, PAE also noted that many students dropped out of their alternative schools. Why? While dropout prevention magnet programs offer a second chance for success to many students on the brink of leaving school, PAE warns that too often students are referred to an alternative program too late to address the harm already done by their schooling. The implications? First, we must offer students a variety of learning opportunities not as a last-ditch effort to "save" vulnerable students but when it first becomes clear that traditional approaches are not working. Second, we must not expect magnet programs to "repair" students only to send them back into the situation that repeatedly fails to meet their needs. Real alternatives must represent a genuine, continuing option for students rather than a "fix-them-and-send-them-back" approach. (p. 4)

If such full-scale programs did exist at the elementary school level, I suspect that both educators and parents would be reluctant to assign a student to these programs. Their reluctance would be understandable for three reasons. First, as has been pointed out many times in this book, there is a stigma attached to alternative education. Second, as we have also previously seen, a large percentage of all alternative schools are alternative in name only. Third, once a student enters an alternative program it may be extremely difficult for her or him to return successfully to the mainstream.

This third point requires additional explanation. On several occasions I have been consulted by districts that were interested in establishing an alternative program at the middle school level. These proposed programs would accept at-risk students. One of the first questions that I asked was, "What happens to these students when they graduate from middle school?" Their answer was that because the high schools in these districts had no alternative school, students would enter a traditional ninth grade classroom. I explained that it may be better to offer no alternative program at all at the middle school level than to offer a middle school program and then require students to return to a traditional program in high school. I have heard hundreds of students in alternative programs say that they "could never go back" to a traditional school. Students who attend successful alternative programs become accustomed to a different culture, a different set of relationships, and a different set of expectations. Because I believe that the problem lies within the system as opposed to the student, to require a student who has attended an alternative school to return to a traditional program (where she or he had previously experienced a cycle of failure) is to perpetuate that cycle of failure.

Should we offer full-fledged alternative programs at the elementary level? For those students who have been identified as most at risk, I think full-fledged alternative elementary programs are a good idea—assuming that an alternative educational system is in place right through Grade 12 and that students who choose to remain in the alternative system are permitted to do so.


## 10. Middle School Model

At the middle school level, at-risk behavior becomes far more apparent. As a result, there begin to appear real alternative programs modeled on one of the prototypes already discussed in this chapter. By an overwhelming majority, the most common middle school alternative is the school-within-a school model.

Dawson (1987) lists 10 components of a comprehensive program to help at-risk middle school students:

1. A formalized identification process
2. A schoolwide discipline program

3. A three-year homeroom class

4. A "secret pal" program (pairs adult mentors with at-risk youth)

5. A dynamic youth services team (makes recommendations for intervening with at-risk youth)

6. An early work experience program

7. A "Gram" program (handwritten notes sent home about positive situations involving students)

8. Administrative and counseling duties are assigned specifically to guarantee "shoe-leather" counseling and contact time

9. A comprehensive retention intervention program (designed to reduce the number of students who must be retained)

10. Firmly established goals for the school. (Dawson, 1987, p. 85)

Because of their age, middle school students generally lack the maturity to handle the openness of the college, mall, or schools-without-walls models. Thus, although there are significant drawbacks to the school-within-a-school model, this model may be suitable for middle school students. The level of "cultural clash" between the alternative middle school program and the traditional middle school program should be substantially less than the clash that can result between alternative and traditional programs at the high school level.

Two points should be emphasized concerning the middle school model. First, despite what research indicates, the majority of districts routinely retain at-risk students in elementary school. As a result, I am familiar with many middle school alternative programs that are filled with 16-, 17-, and 18-year-olds. Until I began working with at-risk secondary students, I didn't realize that there are actually middle school students who drive to school and who are only a few years younger than some of their teachers.

Sadly, for many of these adolescents by the time they enter an alternative program it may be too late and the likelihood of their quitting school is high. I still remember a conversation with one 18-year-old freshman who attended a program that I administered. Recalling his time in an alternative middle school, this young man said, "I ruled eighth grade. The only problem was they hassled me about driving to school."

If you're going to establish an alternative middle school, involve personnel from the elementary schools in the project and do all you can to put an end to the pernicious practice of retaining at-risk students in the primary grades.

Second, involve personnel from the high school in the project and do all you can to establish an alternative program on the high school level, too. Depending on their level of risk, many students who attend an alternative middle school will need an alternative program when they enter high school.

# 5

# How to Set Up
# an Alternative Program

*When I was charged with starting our district's alternative school, I had
no idea of what I was getting into. I expected the kids to be difficult—and
they were. But organizationally, the experience was almost overwhelming.
When you're starting a new school, you don't want to reinvent the wheel.
So I read whatever I could find, made some phone calls, and visited a couple
of alternative schools. The problem was that I didn't find much in the
literature. Most of the alternative schools I visited were schools-within-
schools that had little to distinguish them from traditional school programs. I didn't have much time to plan the program either . . . about two
months. I didn't even get to hire my own staff. The central office reassigned
them to the alternative school from other positions. Some of the teachers
couldn't handle the kids. I ran the alternative school for 3 years . . . the
longest 3 years of my life. When the opportunity came for me to move to
another administrative position, I jumped at the chance. I would never try
to put together another alternative school.*

—a former administrator of a
Pennsylvania alternative high school

To avoid the kind of negative experience described above, you'll
need a comprehensive plan that will address the most important
issues of setting up your program. Many of these issues are discussed

in other chapters of *How to Establish an Alternative School*. The following overview presents key information in abbreviated form.

# 1. Planning

You should form a program planning and management committee at least 1 year before you intend to open your alternative school. This committee should include representatives from all significant groups that will be impacted by the program. I cannot emphasize enough the point that broad-based community support is necessary in order to establish an effective alternative school.

In districts or consortiums of districts that hope to establish an alternative program in one of the more desirable sites (college campus, shopping mall, or school without walls), one of the most common mistakes that occurs at this initial stage is to fail to include significant representation from the planned host site. On many occasions I have been asked by consortiums of districts that wish to establish programs on sites owned or operated by other organizations to participate in these initial planning meetings. Typically, when I walk into the room and am introduced to everyone I discover that the ratio of the number of people representing the school districts to the number of people representing the planned host site is at least 15 : 1. Sitting at the conference table, there are two or three administrators from each school district. There is usually only one representative from the college, mall, shopping district, or school-without-walls sites. Moreover, the individual representing the possible alternative school site rarely has real power in the organization. The effort to establish an innovative program at a desirable site often collapses at this initial stage because of a failure to include significant representation from the impacted site(s). Remember, if you hope to establish an alternative school on someone's else's site, they will almost certainly be negatively impacted to some extent by the program. In order for the host site to accept this negative impact, they must feel a sense of involvement and program "ownership."

What do I mean by "significant representation" from the host site? Significant representation should include people who have real power in all organizations that will be impacted by the program. Membership on the program planning and management committee should not be limited to or dominated by school personnel. For example, if you want to establish a college-based model, there should be a representative from the president's office, the dean of students, influential college faculty, and representatives from the college security and physical plant departments.

Is this process necessarily democratic? No. Do not ask the program planning and management committee to design the entire program. Once you have the authority from the appropriate organization(s) to proceed with the establishment of the alternative school, request that members of the planning and management committee assist with implementation of the kind of program that *you* believe, based upon research and other information gathering processes, will best meet the needs of the district and students.

Readers may interpret some of this advice as contradictory to previous suggestions that staff, students, parents, and the community should be integrally involved in program planning. For several reasons, it is important that a representative group be involved in program planning *but not in program design.* The problem with involving a diverse group in designing the alternative school is that very few individuals have an adequate background in alternative education that would allow them to do so. Involving a large number of individuals in this effort will likely result in long and usually nonproductive discussions on issues such as should the program be punitive versus nonpunitive. (You already know the answer to that question.)

Here's an example of how this process might work. Based upon research that you've conducted and a local needs assessment, you've decided that you want to establish a mentor program. Depending upon the interests of members, the planning and management committee can be divided into various subcommittees. You can ask one of the subcommittees to help establish a mentor program and to recruit qualified individuals from the community.

## 2. Population

You'll have to decide the nature of the population that the program will serve. Assuming that your population will consist of at-risk students, I would recommend that both disruptive and disaffected students be admitted to the program. The disaffected population could include students whose life situations (child care, necessity to work full-time, etc.) are such that they cannot meet the attendance requirements of a traditional school.

The student population should be evenly divided between males and females. I know of several alternative schools that are almost entirely male, despite districts' legitimate need for an alternative programs for females. These all-male programs originate because students are assigned to them by administrators as a result of having committed acts of violence, intimidation, insubordination, and vandalism—offenses that are more likely to be committed by males. There are two serious problems with all-male alternative schools. First, the dynamics of an all-male alternative school class or school are negatively skewed by the absence of females. Second, the needs of at-risk females in the district may be ignored.

The impact upon the site should also be considered when deciding upon the students whom you intend to accept. To illustrate, a college-based program may accept a different population than a self-standing alternative school in an isolated location. Programs should also be racially and ethnically diverse.

## 3. Student Selection Process

You'll need to decide the process through which students will be admitted to the program. When the alternative school is located on another organization's site (college campus, mall, etc.), it's advisable to include representatives from the site on the selection committee. A three-step process is suggested in this case. Step 1 involves screening and recommendation by the traditional school staff. Step 2 involves an interview by the alternative school staff. Step 3 involves review and recommendation by the selection committee, which should consist of representatives from the district, the host site, social service agencies, local and county government, the business community, and the community at large.

## 4. District Support and Resources

The district should be prepared to provide financial, personnel, logistical, and technological support that is equivalent to the level of support provided for students in a traditional school. It's not unusual for alternative schools to be started with grant funding, which may be provided by an outside organization as "seed money" to encourage the establishment of the program. Regardless of whether the alternative school is started with "hard" or "soft" money, in order to ensure program continuity it's important that the alternative school quickly move to the same funding base and level as traditional schools in the same district.

## 5. Site

The following advice seems so obvious that you may question why I give it. Nevertheless, *if at all possible don't begin planning your program until you have a firm commitment as to site.* A surprising number of alternative schools are established, staff hired, curriculum developed, and students accepted before the site has even been determined. This kind of backwards planning usually occurs when grant money has been secured to establish an alternative school, the district has a limited amount of time in which to open the school, and negotiations with an outside agency (which controls access to a desirable site) may be proceeding slowly. (See Chapter 3 for additional information on the importance of site.)

## 6. Staffing

I don't believe that there is any academic background that can adequately prepare a teacher to work with at-risk students. There is, however, life experience that may make one candidate more qualified to work with this population. If you staff the alternative program with appropriate personnel, a very difficult assignment—the day-to-day instruction of at-risk students—will become manageable, perhaps even enjoyable. Place personnel who are unsuited to work with disruptive and disaffected students in the classroom and you'll create the potential for chaos and disaster.

Aside from the required academic credentials and certifications, seek out candidates who are flexible, patient, autonomous, and able to function successfully in a continuously stressful environment. There is mounting evidence that effective schools—particularly effective alternative schools—succeed in creating a sense of "family" among students, faculty, and administration. All staff members, regardless of their position, should also serve as unofficial counselors. Teachers, as well as other staff members, must accept responsibility for the development of the whole adolescent. (See Chapter 3 for additional information on staffing issues.)

## 7. Curriculum

As you plan the curriculum, be sure to include and consider the following information or components:

curriculum/proficiencies
instructional component
personal development
vocational/employment component
community resources
integration of social services
integration of health care providers
program strategies
program goals and objectives
student/teacher ratio

The curriculum should be comprehensive, developed by staff and students to match local needs and interests, hands-on, and include continuous opportunities to integrate cognitive and affective objectives. (See Chapter 6 for a detailed discussion of curriculum issues.)

## Summary

You can use the items included in this chapter as a checklist of the most important issues that you must address in setting up your own program. Remember that although these items have been presented in an abbreviated form, the amount of time and the level of expertise involved in establishing an effective program will be substantial. Hundreds of administrators have visited alternative programs that I've administered to find out how to start their own programs. I've often compared starting an alternative school to lifting an enormous weight. In the first few years, you're simply trying to survive . . . to lift that enormous weight. For whatever the reason (and I suspect that it has to do with the establishment of an alternative school culture and norms, which will take several years to accomplish), it seems that the first few years' problems—fights, suicide attempts, and similar serious incidents—are much more prevalent than the problems that occur during later years.

You have so many "nuts-and-bolts" issues to resolve you probably won't have time for grant writing, publication of a newsletter, or many of the other ideas that I mention in other chapters of *How to Establish an Alternative School*. Don't let that discourage you. In my first few weeks as principal of the Atlantic County Alternative High School (which I founded), I had to deal with several fights, property damage, thefts, and three girls who got so drunk that they vomited in the college cafeteria, passed out, and had to be taken to the emergency room by ambulance. The remainder of that first year was even rougher!

Though the first few years can be extremely difficult, trust me when I tell you that it gets easier. Once the survival of the program is no longer in doubt, you will move to ensure the institutionalization and growth of the alternative school. You can use the checklist in this chapter to get started.

# 6

# Exploring Curriculum Options

Establishing an effective curriculum in an alternative program can be an imposing task. For starters, you'll need to offer English, math, science, social studies, and physical education/health. If resources permit, you may want to offer electives such as foreign languages, art, music, career development, as well as vocational-technical courses. Given the population that you'll be working with, courses will need to be high interest, perceived by students as relevant, and even fun!

Considering the social problems of the students who attend alternative schools, you can't ignore issues such as suicidal ideation, peer mediation, driver education, AIDS and sexually transmitted diseases, and drug and alcohol abuse.

Before beginning our discussion of alternative school curriculum, it's important to understand the reasons why adolescents drop out of school.

## Why Students Quit School:
## The Mismatch Between School and Students' Lives

Many researchers have investigated the reasons that students quit school. Wircenski et al. (1990) write,

A 1983 report by the National Center for Education Statistics listed the reasons given by young people who had dropped out of school and the percentage of each:

| | |
|---|---|
| School not for them | 33.1 percent |
| Poor grades | 33 |
| Offered job or chose to work | 18 |
| Marriage | 17.8 |
| Didn't get along with teachers | 15.5 |
| Had to support family | 11.1 |
| Pregnancy | 10.9 |

Taking into account that these are student-reported reasons, it still is evident that a poor fit of school and student was most often involved in these decisions to leave school. Low grades, a year or more behind grade level, negative school attitudes, and a history of delinquent behavior are noted in the school records of many dropouts. (p. 2)

Hahn (1987) reports that,

A variety of studies have identified the following 10 conditions as major risk factors indicating that a student might be in danger of dropping out.

1. Behind in grade level and older than classmates
2. Poor academic performance
3. Dislike school
4. Detention and suspension
5. Pregnancy
6. Welfare recipients and members of single-parent households
7. The attractiveness of work
8. The attraction of military service
9. Undiagnosed learning disabilities and emotional problems
10. Language difficulties (p. 258)

If you talk with enough at-risk students, you'll find that very few of them really want to quit school. A sizable percentage, however, believe that school "isn't for them." The problem is frequently a reflection of the poor "fit" between what schools offer and what students say they want and need. The program of studies that you develop should meet students' needs—both real and perceived.

I like to define *curriculum* in a very general sense as *the totality of what happens to students in school.* For the most part, what happens to at-risk students in a traditional school is not a very good experience. As a result, at-risk students may either quit school or wind up attending an alternative school, where they are more likely to experience success.

Also, at-risk students tend to devote an inordinate amount of effort to achieving short-term goals, such as saving enough money to buy a car. They will sacrifice more important long-term goals (completing high school) in order to reach their short-term goals. Alternative schools should offer flexible schedules that allow students to achieve short-term goals, without having to sacrifice their education. Regardless of the schedule worked out for a student, the responsibility for meeting learning objectives is placed on the student.

In Chapter 3, I listed 10 characteristics of effective alternative programs. One of these characteristics is curriculum. From my experience, even among some of the more effective alternative schools, the curriculum leaves much to be desired. The curriculum in many alternative programs is frequently just a slightly modified version of the traditional school curriculum. And modified often means "watered down."

Edwards (1989) establishes five conditions that schools need to meet in order to successfully redesign learning and curriculum:

> If schools are to avoid becoming an impediment to students and putting them at-risk, sweeping changes must be made in the way they operate. First, learning must be placed within a cultural and tool-using context. This will involve activity-oriented learning with real problems and phenomena. Second, children must be empowered through development of higher-level thinking skills to deal with problems and conditions in their lives. They must successfully learn how to confront complex, contradictory situations and make proper resolutions. Third, teachers and other school personnel must accept children as they are and give them the necessary experiences to help them become responsibly autonomous. Fourth, the debilitating

system of competition must be eliminated and replaced with a system that is essentially cooperative in nature. Schools are presently one of the few places in society where cooperating is categorically discouraged. However, success in other areas of society often depends on one's ability to cooperate. Fifth, it is imperative that children be given an increasing level of autonomy as they become more able to responsibly make their own decisions. Autonomy needs to include self-regulation as well as curriculum determination. (p. 61)

## A Framework for Curriculum Development

Any curriculum development project should begin with a review of the classic work in the field by Benjamin S. Bloom (1956), *Taxonomy of Educational Objectives*. Bloom lists six cognitive and five affective categories in his hierarchy, shown in Table 6.1. I've included Bloom's taxonomy because the curricula of many alternative schools can be criticized because of a failure to emphasize higher-order thinking skills. In addition, the development of affective skills is often not included in a systematic matter in the alternative school curricula. Critical thinking should be taught across the curriculum, through a variety of complex, cognitive activities, including

solving problems,
generating and organizing ideas,
forming and applying concepts,
designing systematic plans of action,
constructing and evaluating arguments,
exploring issues from multiple perspectives,
applying knowledge to new situations,
critically evaluating the logic and validity of information,
developing evidence to support views,
carefully analyzing situations,
discussing subjects in an organized way.

In developing a curriculum, you should keep in mind that when working with at-risk students *how* you deliver the curriculum is

**Table 6.1**  Bloom's Cognitive and Affective Categories

---

*Cognitive Domain*

1.0  Knowledge
　　1.1  Knowledge of specifics
　　1.2  Knowledge of ways and means of dealing with specifics
　　1.3  Knowledge of universals and abstractions in a field
2.0  Comprehension
　　2.1  Translation
　　2.2  Interpretation
　　2.3  Extrapolation
3.0  Application
4.0  Analysis
　　4.1  Analysis of elements
　　4.2  Analysis of relationships
　　4.3  Analysis of organizational principles
5.0  Synthesis
　　5.1  Production of unique communication
　　5.2  Production of a plan or proposed set of operations
　　5.3  Derivation of a set of abstract relations
6.0  Evaluation
　　6.1  Judgment in terms of intended evidence
　　6.2  Judgment in terms of external criteria

*Affective Domain*

1.0  Receiving (attending)
　　1.1  Awareness
　　1.2  Willingness to receive
　　1.3  Controlled or selected attention
2.0  Responding
　　2.1  Acquiescence in responding
　　2.2  Willingness to respond
　　2.3  Satisfaction in response
3.0  Valuing
　　3.1  Acceptance of a value
　　3.2  Preference for a value
　　3.3  Commitment
4.0  Organization
　　4.1  Conceptualization of a value
　　4.2  Organization of a value system
5.0  Characterization by a value or value complex
　　5.1  Generalized set
　　5.2  Characterization

---

SOURCE: Adapted from Bloom (1956).

almost as important as *what* curriculum you deliver. Remember that with at-risk students, affective development usually precedes cognitive growth. Curricula must be developed that consistently integrates the cognitive and affective domains across all subject areas. The curriculum should be hands-on; students' feelings of self-worth and accomplishment should be nurtured by the work itself; and academic assignments should be integrally related to real work in the real world.

## Developing the Core Curriculum

It's a good idea to visit several alternative schools before you start your own program. *It's not a good idea, though, to simply import a curriculum from another school—whether alternative or traditional.* Nevertheless, this is what often occurs when a new program is started. Within certain broad parameters, the staff and students should be permitted substantial input into the development of the alternative school course of studies. Education is more successful when the teacher and the student agree on the learning materials, how these materials are to be used, and the expected outcomes. In some programs, expectations are recorded in contracts that stipulate goals, outcomes, learning materials, and time lines. Again, within very broad parameters, teachers and students should be allowed to select textbooks and materials that they agree upon, as well as the method of the material's presentation (written, verbal, computer-assisted, etc.). Time should be provided for reflection upon important life questions. The importance of reading and writing across the curriculum should be emphasized.

Knapp, Shields, and Turnbull (1990) write,

> The available evidence suggests that effective curriculum should: (1) focus on meaning and understanding from the beginning—for example, by orienting instruction toward comprehending reading passages, communicating important ideas in written text, or understanding the concepts underlying number facts; (2) balance routine skill learning with novel and complex tasks from the earliest stages of learning; (3) provide a context for skill learning that establishes clear reasons for needing to learn the skills, affords opportunities to apply the skills, and helps students relate one skill to another; (4) influence attitudes and beliefs about the academic content areas, as well as skills and knowledge;

(5) eliminate unnecessary redundancy in the curriculum (e.g., repeated instruction in the same mathematics computations year after year). (p. 5)

## Credit Awarding: Time-Based Versus Proficiency-Based Tracks

You'll actually need to establish two curricula in your alternative school. Because of students' need for a flexible program of studies, you should develop a proficiency-based program, as well as a time-based model (the method in which credits are awarded in a traditional school). Depending upon her needs, a student may be placed on a 100% time-based model (which means that the student attends classes for all or most of the day); a 100% proficiency-based model (which means that a student does not attend classes but is placed on a program of independent study and meets with teachers to turn in assignments and take examinations); or some combination of a time-based and proficiency-based program.

In order to be placed on a proficiency-based program, a student should demonstrate that a legitimate need (employment, child care, participation in an externship, performance of community service, etc.) prevents her from attending regularly scheduled classes. The activities of students who are placed on a proficiency-based program should be closely monitored by school staff. If a student is complying with the stipulations of the proficiency-based program that has been established, she should be recorded as present in school. If a student fails to meet the requirements of the proficiency-based program, she should be required to return to school where she will be placed in a time-based program of classes.

Under a proficiency-based program, students can also earn credits by successful completion of a comprehensive examination that demonstrates mastery of locally determined proficiencies, including, but not limited to, the statewide core proficiencies in a curricula area for which credit is awarded.

## Individualized Program Plan

An individualized program plan (IPP) should be developed for each student. The development of this plan should include input from the students, parents, and the alternative school staff. This plan provides a record of each student's course of study and a rationale to explain why a particular course of study or credit-awarding option (time-based, proficiency-based, or mastery examination) was selected. The IPP should also include information about the student's current educational performance, including academic achievement, specific behavioral and educational objectives to be addressed, vocational aspirations, and plans for employment or continuing education following graduation from high school. In addition, it's important that a file be maintained for any student who will receive credits based upon successful completion of a program of independent study or mastery examination. In this file you should include a record of all work completed while a student is on independent study, including copies of quizzes, tests, examinations, papers, projects, and so forth. The materials in this file will provide evidence to critics— and there will be critics of any nontraditional credit-awarding arrangement—that students who have earned credits under nontraditional arrangements are completing "real" academic work.

## The Role of Technology in the Curriculum

Technology should be a critical component of the curriculum and needs to be integrated throughout the entire alternative school program. Perhaps more than any other group of students, at-risk adolescents should be provided access to the "information superhighway."

Catello and Peck (1990) write,

Instructional media and educational technology offer powerful tools for the ark builders. Several locations across the United States are in the process of proving how media-intensive programs can capture the attention and interest of at-risk students. By providing appropriate, interactive instruction, these programs can improve attitudes, keep young people in school, and make a significant contribution to the total educational environment, producing measurable academic achievements. . . . Instructional materials identified included videotapes, computer-assisted instruction, satellite broadcasts, interactive video-based modules, CDROM databases, hands-on experiments and demonstrations. (p. 54)

## Other Important Curriculum Issues

Aside from instruction in core subjects such as English, math, science, social studies, and physical education and health, you should include several other components in the curriculum.

### *Crisis Intervention and Suicide Prevention*

Statistics indicate that there are as many as 7,000 deaths and 400,000 suicide attempts among the 15- to 24-year-old age groups. Because many suicides are not reported or are called accidents, the actual number of suicide and suicide attempts is believed to be higher. The number seven cause of deaths among 5- to 14-year-olds in the United States, suicide increases dramatically among 15- to 24-year-olds and is the number two cause of death for this age group. The percentage of completed suicides has increased 300% since the 1960s. Every day, 11 teenagers will commit suicide. That's one suicide death every 2 hours and 15 minutes. A study of California secondary school students reported that 38% of all students had contact with a friend who had talked about suicide or had made a suicide attempt. Among at-risk students, the likelihood for suicide is significantly greater. An effective school-based suicide prevention program should include information such as the following:

suicide statistics

warning signs

developing problem-solving skills

improving communication skills

where to find help

All students and staff should be trained to recognize the five warning signs of suicide, as identified by the American Association of Suicidology: (a) a suicide threat or indication of a desire or intent to die; (b) a previous suicide attempt; (c) significant behavioral changes, including changes in eating or sleeping patterns, hyperactivity, substance abuse, and involvement in high risk-taking behavior; (d) depression; (e) making final arrangements, saying good-bye to friends, and giving away valued possessions.

Schools should not wait until a suicide or suicide attempt has occurred to initiate a suicide prevention program. Units related to suicide prevention should be included as an integral part of the health curriculum, and school personnel and parents should be involved in planning elements of this curriculum. Schools should integrate their efforts with those of community mental health providers. In addition, schools should have a detailed plan to implement should a suicide or suicide attempt occur. All staff members should be familiar with this plan, which will help to safeguard students as well as to protect the school from lawsuits related to possible negligence. A matter-of-fact announcement that a suicide occurred should be made to students by the individual who has been designated to be in charge during a crisis (usually the principal). Individual students should have immediate access to counselors to discuss the feelings of anger, guilt, and fear that are likely to arise. Staff should be aware of information related to communal response to adolescent suicide. The plan should include when parents are to be notified, by whom, and what they will be told.

Suicide prevention efforts should not be limited to the health curriculum. For example, in English class students could be exposed to the issue of suicide in works such as *Romeo and Juliet, Ordinary People, Richard Cory, The Bell Jar,* and *The Dead Poets Society.* Discussions and writing assignments can provide students with an opportunity to voice their feelings about suicide.

With younger children, puppet shows that present general themes of life and death and children's feelings about those themes have proven effective. Through a series of vignettes, the puppets might portray the death of a pet, the separation of parents, or the loss of a friend because of moving or death. Afterwards, teachers lead a discussion on the themes presented in the puppet show.

## Alcohol: Use, Abuse, and Prevention Programs

The use of alcohol among American adolescents has reached epidemic proportions. For large numbers of American teenagers, the weekend belongs to Michelob. The average age that children begin using alcohol is 12 years and 5 months. By the ninth grade, the majority of teenage social affairs include alcohol use. More accepted both socially and legally than an other drug and more readily available, alcohol poses a serious, potentially life-threatening problem for teenagers.

Students view drinking as a social activity, a tension reducer, and reflective of behavior patterns of parents and peers. Many students, who would never consider smoking marijuana or trying cocaine or LSD, do not consider alcohol to be a "drug." In a recent *USA Today* poll of student council leaders, 50% of students indicated that alcohol was their school's number one problem. (In second place at 17% was student apathy.) The U.S. Department of Justice reports that drinking is associated with 27% of all murders committed by young people, 31% of all rapes, and 37% of all robberies.

Alcohol is also the number one "gateway" drug—that is, its consumption may lead to the use and abuse of harder drugs. Teen drinkers are responsible for 50% of all fatal automobile accidents. One half of all high school students are considered regular drinkers, one third drink heavily at least once a week, one quarter have a serious drinking problem, and four million youth under the age of 17 are alcoholics.

Over my 20 years of experience in working with at-risk students, the biggest change that I've seen in the area of substance use and abuse has been a decrease in illicit drug use such as marijuana, cocaine, and LSD and *a dramatic increase* in the use of alcohol, especially among younger students. Because of this increase, groups such as Students Against Drunk Driving (SADD) have been formed on many high school campuses. I have mixed feelings about groups such as SADD. I know of several high schools that have prohibited the establishment of SADD chapters because they unintentionally may water down the message that teens should not drink at all. Certainly, no one wants a teenager to drink and then get behind the steering wheel. There seems an implicit assumption in the SADD message, however: that it's OK for teenagers to drink—just don't drink and drive. Polls indicate that many teenagers seem to believe just that—drinking is a normal part of the adolescent experience, but drinking and driving don't mix.

It's clear that every school needs a program that addresses alcohol use, abuse, and prevention. For alternative schools the need is even greater, because the majority of at-risk students abuse alcohol. In the preceding paragraph I mentioned that some high schools will not allow SADD chapters to form because they may transmit the wrong message to students. In planning your school's alcohol education program, you'll have to decide to teach either that teenagers should not drink at all (the traditional message), or, if teens choose to drink they should learn how to drink responsibly. There is no national consensus on this issue. Some argue that we must reject the idea of teaching the responsible use of alcohol. Because alcohol use is illegal for those under 21, schools should not and cannot teach teenagers how to responsibly use an illegal substance. Others argue that because alcohol use is so ingrained into American society and adolescent culture, schools have a moral obligation to teach students to use it in a responsible manner.

Given the important role of alcohol in adolescent culture, particularly the culture of at-risk adolescents, I recommend that your alcohol education program help teenagers—if they choose to drink at all—to develop a more responsible attitude toward alcohol. St. Pierre and Miller (1986) propose an eight-step model of responsible use of alcoholic beverages among teenagers.

1. Avoid drunkenness.
2. Respect the personal decisions of others who choose to drink or abstain.
3. Use positive adult models to shape the drinking patterns of young people.
4. Present factual information concerning alcohol and its effects on the body.
5. Promote awareness, a sensitivity to the dynamics of responsibility that envelop the use and nonuse of alcoholic beverages in situational, safety, and health-related environments.
6. Assist young people in adapting to a predominant drinking society.
7. Discourage drinking for its own sake and encourage the integration of drinking with the use of food and other activities.
8. Enhance human dignity through the use of alcoholic beverages.

An intensive education program can cause significant changes in knowledge about alcohol and alcohol-related behavior. The program requires a total school involvement. Effective alcohol education programs should not be limited to health class but should integrate information into the regular curriculum as well.

Two other points are important here. First, among at-risk students, drinking and driving is an especially dangerous problem. Of all age groups, 15- to 19-year-olds have the highest rates of involve-ment in alcohol-related automobile accidents. Because of adolescents' belief in their own immortality—"It won't happen to me!"—pro-grams that rely heavily on scare tactics have limited success. Instead, programs that focus on the friends and peers of high-risk adolescent drivers appear to be more effective. These "Stop the Drinking Driver" kinds of programs involve modeling, the use of positive peer pressure, and assertive skills training. Encouraging social responsi-bility, these programs allow students to practice how to stop the drinking driver and to motivate student use of these techniques when necessary. Second, a certain percentage of students in the alternative program will have such a severe drinking problem that a residential treatment program will be necessary. All staff members should be trained as to how to identify those in the school with the most serious problem and where these students may be referred in order to obtain help.

## Illegal Substance Use, Abuse, and Prevention

In the previous section, I mentioned that substance use among teenagers has been declining while alcohol use was increasing dra-matically. Despite this trend, given the prevalence of cross-addiction among at-risk adolescents, it is likely that many students in your alternative school will use and abuse illegal substances, primarily marijuana, inhalants, cocaine, and hallucinogens such as LSD. Ac-cording to the National Institute on Drug Abuse, 61% of high school seniors have tried illegal drugs. One in 10 high school seniors has tried cocaine. The Bureau of Juvenile Statistics reports that almost half of all juveniles in correctional facilities committed their offenses while under the influence of drugs or alcohol.

Ficklen (1990) lists 12 core concepts that can help schools deter drug use:

1. Do an assessment of your school's drug problem
2. Have a strong, no-drugs policy that offers students a helping hand
3. Make the policy known
4. Follow up with an after care program for those students who violate the policy

5.  Teach a no-use drug message
6.  Provide alternatives to drug use
7.  Incorporate social responsibility into the anti-drug program
8.  Provide mentors for high-risk kids
9.  Include parents and other adults
10. Create alliances with other anti-drug efforts in the area
11. Repeat anti-drug instruction
12. Don't forget "good" kids (pp. 19-22)

Many drug education programs fail to address this issue effectively due to a lack of a comprehensive planning and implementation model. An effective model should include the following five phases: needs assessment, planning process, implementation, evaluation, and dissemination. The cooperation and coordination of many people from both the school and community are needed to make the program work.

Across the United States, there are generally three types of drug education programs: programs that focus on providing factual information about drugs; programs that focus on attitudes and values; and programs that focus more directly on behavior. Programs should be developed that include all three components and that include extensive development of personal and resistance skills.

### Internships and Externships

Many alternative schools arrange internships and externships for students. There arrangements allow students to develop more "hands-on" experience and training in various occupations and careers. The internship and externship program at New York City's Middle College High School is one of the most effective in the United States. Lieberman (1985) writes that,

> The internship program, patterned after the college's cooperative education sequence, develops motivation and a sense of purpose and is a strong factor in keeping adolescents in school. In many cases, the work experience gives students a sense of self-worth. Curricular materials developed in cooperation with the college faculty prepare students for mean-

ingful off-site educational experiences. There is a program of "coop-prep." College level internships are also available for selected Middle College students. Advanced standing credit in co-op is provided for Middle College graduates who attend LaGuardia, and students who successfully complete the internship sequence at Middle College are exempted from the internship if they choose to attend LaGuardia Community College.

Students select internships from: human services, business technology, and liberal arts and sciences. Internships are generally unpaid, but students receive credit towards their high school diploma. These internships are in a variety of governmental agencies, hospitals, schools, and occasionally businesses. (pp. 5-6)

## Peer Mediation and the Development of Conflict Resolution Skills

The statistics concerning violence and vandalism in the nation's public schools are frightening. According to the National Association for Mediation in Education (1990), almost 8% of urban and junior and senior high school students miss at least one day of school a month because they are afraid to go. Each month, 280,000 students are physically attacked in America's secondary schools. Approximately 5,200 secondary school teachers are attacked every month.

According to the U.S. Department of Justice (Kalish, 1988), the rate of violent crime in the United States is 4 times higher than rates in Europe. The U.S. homicide rate is between 8 and 20 times higher than that of other developed countries (Fingerhut & Kleinman, 1990). Half of the households in the United States possess at least one firearm (Wright, Rossi, Daly, & Weber-Burdin, 1983), and there are approximately 200 million guns in this country (Olinger, 1991).

The number of hate crimes has exploded across the United States. In *Hate Crime*, Bodinger-DeUriarte and Sancho (1992) define a hate crime as,

Any act, or attempted act, to cause physical injury, emotional suffering, or property damage through intimidation, harassment, racial/ethnic slurs and bigoted epithets, vandalism, force, or the threat of force, motivated all or in part by hostility to the victim's real or perceived race, ethnicity, religion, or sexual orientation. (p. 54)

## Rationale for Peer Mediation Program

Given the level of violence in the United States, the development of effective conflict resolution skills is as important among students in alternative schools as the development of reading, writing, and math skills. Without these conflict resolutions skills, at-risk adolescents may become involved in serious and potentially life-threatening incidents both in and out of school. The National Association for Mediation in Education (1990) provides the following 10 reasons as a rationale for implementing a school-based mediation program.

1. Conflict is a natural human state often accompanying changes in our institutions or personnel. It is better approached with skills than avoidance.

2. More appropriate and effective systems are needed to deal with conflict in the school setting than expulsion, court intervention, and detention.

3. The use of mediation to resolve school-based disputes can result in improved communication between and among students, teachers, administrators, and parents and can, in general, improve the school climate as well as provide a forum for addressing common concerns.

4. The use of mediation as a conflict resolution method can result in a reduction in violence, vandalism, chronic school absence, and suspension.

5. Mediation training helps both young people and teachers to deepen their understanding about themselves and others and provides them with lifetime dispute resolution skills.

6. Mediation training increases students' interest in conflict resolution, justice, and the American legal system while encouraging a high level of citizenship activity.

7. Shifting the responsibility for solving appropriate school conflicts from adults to young adults and children frees both teachers and administrators to concentrate more on teaching than on discipline.

8. Recognizing that young people are competent to participate in the resolution of their own disputes encourages student growth and gives students skills—such as listening, critical thinking, and problem solving—that are basic to all learning.

9. Mediation training, with its emphasis upon listening to others' points of view and the peaceful resolution of differences, assists in preparing students to live in a multicultural world.

10. Mediation provides a system of problem solving that is uniquely suited to the personal nature of young people's problems and is frequently used by students for problems they would not take to parents, teachers, or principals. (p. 27)

A peer mediation program can be an important part of the alternative school curriculum. According to the National Association for Mediation in Education (1990), school mediation makes a number of assumptions that are at odds with traditional educational philosophy. These assumptions include the following:

1. That conflict is an unavoidable part of living that can be used as an opportunity for student learning and personal growth.

2. That because conflict is unavoidable, learning conflict resolution skills is educational and as essential to the long-term success of young people as learning geometry or history.

3. That students can resolve their conflicts with the assistance of other students as effectively if not more effectively than they can with the assistance of adults.

4. That encouraging disputing students to collaboratively resolve the causes of present conflict is a more effective method for preventing future conflict (and developing student responsibility) than administering punishment for past actions. (p. 27)

## Conclusion

A large number of educators who are interested in starting their own programs have visited alternative schools that I've administered. They invariably have asked for copies of the curriculum. With some reluctance I provide this information, as well as any other written materials that I think may be helpful. My reluctance to provide curriculum materials stems from the fact that the curriculum should be as integral to the school culture as food, water, and oxygen are to the human body. Curriculum development is an ongoing process, continually evolving in response to the needs of the students and community. Though I have provided general principles of alternative school curriculum development in this chapter, remember that curriculum should be developed by the participants—students and staff—at the local school site to meet the specific needs of students in the alternative school.

# 7

# Administering and
# Organizing Alternative Schools

Suggestions on how to administer and organize an alternative
school are contingent upon several variables, the most important
of which are site and administrative leadership. The discussion that
follows concerning the administration and organization of alternative schools is applicable to all alternative programs. Because of the
complexity of the administrative structure, I will initially focus on
administering and organizing programs located on college campuses, in shopping malls, or without walls.

You may recall the general principles that were listed in Chapter
4 on the importance of site. To summarize these principles:

1. The richer the site, the more powerful the effect of the site on
   modifying the cognitive and affective performance of at-risk
   students.
2. The more likely the site is to oppose the establishment of an
   alternative school on its premises.
3. The greater the level of cultural clash that will result when
   at-risk students (many of whom will be members of families
   from a lower socioeconomic background) are integrated into
   the mainstream and come in contact with individuals (many

of whom will be members of families from a middle or upper socioeconomic background) from the host site.

Also, recall that I wrote that the administrator of any school—alternative or traditional—must be an effective political leader, managerial leader, and instructional leader. When a program is located on a very rich site (a college campus, for example), the administrator's most important function is to be a successful political leader who can create and facilitate the structures and processes that will enable the alternative school to survive the "backlash" from the host site culture. This backlash is a necessary by-product of the growth process that occurs when at-risk students are integrated into the core culture of the host site.

## Threefold Administrative Structure
## Required for Highest SES Sites

I've had substantial success in establishing countywide alternative programs on rich sites. On college-based programs with which I've been associated, three separate administrative structures have been necessary. (Variations on the same three-fold administrative arrangement that I'm going to describe in the next several paragraphs should be developed for other complex models, such as mall-based schools or schools without walls.)

### Administrative Relationship
### With the Local Education Agency

The first and easiest administrative structure to establish is the formal structural relationship between the alternative school and the school district or local education agency (LEA) of which the alternative school is a member. The administration of the alternative school should report directly to the superintendent, in the same manner as the principal of any school in the district would report to the superintendent. The local school board (or local governing authority, depending upon the identity of the LEA) should exercise legal and fiscal authority over the alternative school and approve personnel decisions, curriculum for the alternative school, and similar matters.

## Administrative Relationship
## With the Sending Schools

The second administrative structure that is integral to a college-based program consists of the somewhat less formal relationship between the alternative school and the schools that will send students to the program. (Obviously, if the program accepts students from only one district, there will be no need for this second level of administration.) Working together, administrators from each of the sending schools and the principal of the alternative school must develop mutually acceptable policies and procedures that can be applied to a wide range of issues. Some of these issues will include: criteria for admission of students to the alternative school; credit-awarding arrangements; participation of alternative school students in sending school events, such as graduation ceremonies and extra-curricular activities; and discipline of alternative school students who commit an offense on the premises of the sending school.

Though it may be helpful in some situations, it is not necessary that all these policies and procedures be formalized in a written document. In fact, there are some advantages in *not* writing down certain policies and procedures and working some situations out on an informal, case-by-case basis. For example, I can recall hundreds of situations when home school administrators and I informally agreed to waive certain policies or overlook certain inappropriate student behaviors if we believed this to be in the best interest of the student. To illustrate, many times students will enter an alternative school during the course of the school year, after the student has already lost credit for the year in a traditional school due to excessive absences. After consulting with me, the home school administrator may agree to excuse those absences in the traditional school, thus offering a student a "fresh start" at the alternative school.

I can recall many instances when such informal negotiations involved more serious matters. For example, I remember a case when a 17-year-old female who, on the day before she was to start classes at our alternative school, pulled a knife (but did not use it) in the midst of an altercation with another student at the sending school. According to the policy of that school, the student who pulled the knife should have been arrested and expelled. The home school principal called me, informed me of the incident, and asked if I could arrange for some form of punishment for the student—an intelligent, troubled young woman to whom the home school principal wanted to give another chance at the alternative school. The young woman who had pulled the knife was successful in the alternative school, received her high school diploma, and went on to college. (As punishment for the incident with the knife, the student received 10 days in-school suspension at the alternative school.)

Any experienced school administrator—whether that school is alternative or traditional—knows that there are times when you don't necessarily go "by the book." If certain problematic situations are to be worked out informally and on a case-by-case basis, a close relationship characterized by mutual respect and trust must exist between the administrators of the alternative and traditional schools.

Another example of the importance of this relationship involves the student selection process. Although the alternative school staff should interview prospective students and carefully review all pertinent records, including academic, discipline, and health files, it is the administration and staff of the sending school who will be most knowledgeable about the potential of each student. As an administrator of an alternative high school on a college campus, I have had to be extremely careful about accepting students who have committed violent acts and weapons offenses. Imagine the consequences if a student in a college-based alternative school brings a gun to school and fires it on campus. Almost invariably, the college will blame the entire program for the actions of this one student and the alternative school will be removed from the campus setting. (This is not to imply that it is a minor incident if the student fired a gun on the grounds of the traditional school; however, the entire high school will not be closed or forced to relocate because of the behavior of one violent or disturbed student.)

A percentage of students in the college-based programs with which I have been involved had committed serious acts of violence at the home school or on the street, including weapons offenses. These students, however, were able to successfully adapt their behavior to the norms of the college environment and avoid a similar incident on campus. These students were accepted into the alternative school because home school administrators whom I respect and trust believed that these were decent, salvageable adolescents who had made a mistake and deserved a second chance. I should also point out that I am aware of a few programs that were closed or forced to relocate because home school administrators—seeking to remove seriously disturbed adolescents from their building—"dumped" students who did not belong in an alternative setting into the program, and these students subsequently committed a particularly egregious act of violence.

## Administrative Relationship
## With the College, Shopping Mall,
## and School-Without-Walls Sites

The administrative relationship with the college, shopping mall, or schools-without-walls sites is the most complex and important relationship that must be developed. When an outside organization agrees to host an alternative program, a number of complicated issues arise. These issues concern matters such as the availability and cost of classroom and office space; the use of host site technology and recreational facilities; and the behavior of alternative school students. Because these issues all revolve around an outside organization—the alternative school, which is generally perceived as a negative entity—that seeks to utilize the resources of another, larger and more politically powerful organization, they are intrinsically political in nature. The resolution of these issues requires superior political skills on the part of the alternative school administrator. The alternative school administrator must also have political support from above— meaning at the level of the superintendent, school board, and local, county, and even state government, depending upon the geographical scope of the program.

In the early 1990s, the New Jersey Department of Education embarked upon an ambitious program to locate alternative schools for chronically disruptive students, including adolescents who had been released from county and state correctional facilities, on college campuses throughout the state. Based to a considerable extent upon the success of the program (the state's first college-based alternative high school) that I had established in 1986 on the campus of Atlantic Community College in Mays Landing, New Jersey, the New Jersey Department of Education became convinced that college-based alternative schools were the most effective means available to rescue at-risk youth and to divert adolescents from acts of juvenile delinquency. Because of my experience in establishing a successful college-based model, I was called upon on many occasions to give presentations or consultations to groups that were interested in establishing an alternative school on a college campus. I spoke to many groups throughout the state. In almost every instance, colleges were opposed (sometimes adamantly) to proposals to situate alternative high schools for the chronically disruptive on their campuses. In every single situation in which a college opposed the establishment of an alternative school on its campus, the same excuse was given: "We would love to help you out, but our college simply has no space available for your program."

What the college representatives were really saying was this—"We actually have space available, but we do not consider your program important enough to provide you with the space that you've requested." This is the old NIMBY (Not In My Backyard) argument. In several instances, after political persuasion—and sometimes pressure—was brought to bear upon the college, they were somehow able to come up with space for these programs.

I don't mean to criticize these colleges for their reluctance to permit alternative schools to be established on their campuses, or for their less-than-candid explanation as to why they were reluctant to allow these schools to be situated on their premises. What else could colleges say?—that these alternative kids can be rude, insolent, intimidating, obnoxious, and even dangerous and that we'd be crazy to "want" those kinds of people on campus. I've seen the same scenario when malls and potential school-without-walls sites have been approached concerning the establishment of an alternative school on their premises.

The point I want to emphasize is that this is a political situation, involving the allocation and utilization of scarce resources. Thus, the administrator of one of these alternative models must be—above anything else—a successful political leader. The basic principle of success in administering such programs involves the inclusion of all significant constituencies (including rational opponents) in the governance of the alternative program.

## What About Less Complicated Programs?

Less complicated models (school-within-a-school, after school programs, etc.) require less political effort on the part of the administrator. I've administered a few of these models as well. Though these models generally have less impact upon students, the administrator can devote more time and energy to instructional and managerial matters. This does not mean that the administrator can ignore political issues. Remember that many schools-within-a school—the most prevalent of all alternative models—begin as full-time day programs. As a result of the conflict created by the "two sets of rules within the same building" problem, however (a conflict that has political implications), day programs wind up being rescheduled as after school programs.

## Authoritarian Versus Democratic Organizational Structure

Regardless of the location of the program, the administrative structure should be democratic, as opposed to the traditional authoritarian structure that characterizes most schools. Because alternative schools are often involved with many other schools, programs, agencies, and so forth, there is a natural tendency for busy administrators toward an authoritarian organizational leadership style. This trend will be exacerbated as enrollment increases. This tendency, however, must be resisted. (In a similar manner, there is a trend for alternative schools to become more traditional with the passage of time.) This is not to suggest that administrators should not be "in charge"; however, a power with—rather than a power over—approach to administration is required. I've administered both traditional and alternative schools. Without question, I've found that the administration of an alternative school involves greater organizational skill, energy, and resourcefulness.

Comer (1987) writes,

School organization and management have been hierarchial and authoritarian, even while the corporations and other organizations have been moving toward shared power, collaboration, and cooperation to address relationship issues relevant to their mission. In schools today the teaching and learning mission requires collaboration. Hierarchial and authoritarian organizations are unable to create a supportive climate at the service delivery or school building level because this structure cannot adjust easily to groups or individuals with needs different from those of the majority. For this reason, children from families under stress, children who are underdeveloped, or those who are less likely to learn and behave as expected are at greater risk in the school structure. The sources of risk, therefore, are *in* the schools, as well as in societal and family conditions outside the school. (p. 14)

## Systems Thinking and Contingency Management

A "systems approach" is useful when administrating and organizing an alternative school. A systems approach means that all parts are interrelated and interdependent to form a whole. A system is composed of components or subsystems that are related to or dependent on one another. A systems approach calls for a integrative contingency approach to managing—as opposed to the utilization of traditional "organizational" principles, which are supposed to hold regardless of the situation or condition. Contingency approaches involve relationships that hold for clearly specified circumstances or conditions. As circumstances or conditions change, the managerial or organizational approach will adapt.

Describing a collaboration effort between the New Haven, Connecticut Public Schools and the Yale Child Study Center for School Development, Comer (1987) writes,

> We intervened at the systems level, acknowledging that the school building is a modifiable social system and one that is as much a potential factor in continued student underdevelopment as are the students, families, and community. It is a process model in which administrators, parents, teachers, and support staff work collaboratively through three mechanisms: a governance and management group, a mental health group or support staff group, and a parents' group. The goal is to create a social climate that helps to close the student development gap, to create an academic program based on achievement data, and to carry out a staff development program based on social and academic goals established at the building level. The coordinating element is the governance and management group, which, with the support of the school staff, develops and carries out a compressive building plan to address school social climate, academic performance, and staff development. (p. 15)

The alternative school administrator should ensure that teachers and students have the autonomy to develop their own program, rather than have a program or curriculum imposed by the school district.

The Hofstra University Center for the Study of Educational Alternatives lists the following features as contributing to the probable *failure* of a new alternative program:

1.  It is designed by administrators, not its staff.
2.  It is imported from somewhere else and set into operation, pretty much intact, as it worked elsewhere.
3.  The program is a referral program to which students are assigned.
4.  The alternative is a last chance program which a student must choose in order to avoid suspension or expulsion.
5.  The program is punitive in orientation.
6.  The alternative is built around a single cluster of new elements—perhaps a new curriculum or a new set of activities—but holds all other features of school operation intact and unmodified.
7.  The alternative is treated just as any new department within the school—or new school within the district—might be. It is expected to conform to existing regulations, operating procedures, and arrangements.
8.  Staff are assigned to the alternative by administrators outside it—or by automatic processes such as contract rights.
9.  The alternative is intended for the toughest classes—and designed to reflect the absolutely minimal departures from traditional school practice to accommodate them.
10. No one in the district is told very much about the new program and guidance counselors are left to remain lukewarm about it. (cited in Sweeney & Wheelock, 1989, p. 6)

I don't necessarily agree with two of these statements: Numbers 3 and 4. In Chapter 3, I wrote that sometimes an administrator has no choice but to assign a student to an alternative school. I think the other items on the list are absolutely correct, however.

There is no "top down" prescription that will guarantee the success of a new alternative school. Nevertheless, the administrator should work to institutionalize diversity and choice and to provide common planning time for teachers, who need to become reflective practitioners.

Because of the needs of students, the environment of an alternative program can appear to be in an almost continual state of change. The informal culture of alternative schools also contributes to a perception (sometimes a criticism) that some have that alternative programs are "structure-less." The fact is that effective alternative schools may *appear* structure-less; however, in order to respond to the many significant problems that at-risk students bring to the classroom, alternative programs that work are precisely organized. This precise degree of organization facilitates flexibility and change (a strength of systems thinking) rather than inhibits them. It is the responsibility of the administrator to create the structural foundation that supports the alternative school, at the same time making sure that this structural foundation remains as "invisible" as possible. Systems thinking and contingency-based management approaches will facilitate this process.

# 8

# Empowering Teachers

*This is only my second year teaching . . . both years in the same alternative school. Sometimes I didn't think I was going to make it through my first year. College and student teaching didn't begin to prepare me for what I have to face every day in my classroom. Sometimes I feel like I'm responsible for everything that happens to these kids—not just when they're in school but for lives outside of school, too. Relationships with their parents are generally so adversarial that a lot of these kids don't have any responsible adults to talk to, except the staff here at the alternative school. In addition to teaching history, I spend a lot of time talking about dating, birth control, drinking and drugs, jobs, driving . . . you name it. When I was hired, the principal told me that everybody on the staff, regardless of their position, was both a teacher and a counselor and that if I developed the right kind of relationship with students they would bring their personal problems to me. That's exactly what happened. The principal also told me that I would have to create my own structure inside my classroom. He said that the traditional structures, mechanisms, and processes that support teachers in traditional schools weren't a part of the alternative school culture . . . I have almost complete autonomy in textbook selection and the material that I cover and how I cover that material in my courses. I love teaching at the alternative school . . . I feel like I'm making a bigger difference in kids' lives teaching here than if I were teaching at a traditional high school. Still, I have so much autonomy, so much responsibility . . . it can be overwhelming at times.*

—Gail, a second-year English teacher at
a New Jersey alternative high school

The term *at risk* invokes frustration in some teachers and sympathy in others. Teachers of at-risk youth can easily become discouraged and overwhelmed and begin to wonder if their efforts are all in vain. Students in alternative schools are capable of burning out their teachers over a surprisingly short period of time, if these teachers are not prepared to cope with the serious problems that these young people bring to the classroom.

Jennings and Nathan (1977) write,

> Alternative school staffs and parents sometimes become disheartened or discouraged. Often they expect all problems to be solved by establishing a new structure or organization. It is vital that people not confuse the value of the ideas and techniques they are using with difficulties they have in actually carrying them out. Working with young people is hard work, and we always know more than we are able to do at any particular moment. Still, most surviving experimental or alternative schools find that their programs get better and better and that the student/parent satisfaction increases steadily. (p. 572)

## A Paradigm Shift

Teachers in alternative schools need to undergo a fundamental paradigm shift. This shift will enable teachers to become the foci of influence in their classrooms and to understand that regardless of their students' level of dysfunction, they can successfully intervene and help students make cognitive and affective progress. Such a shift is integral to the process of "empowerment," which Melenyzer (1993) defines as "the opportunity and confidence to act upon one's ideas and to influence the way one performs in one's profession. True empowerment leads to increased professionalism as teachers assume responsibility for an involvement in the decision making process" (p. 3).

The remainder of this chapter discusses ways to empower teachers.

### Initiating Shared Governance

Based upon what you're read to this point in *How to Establish an Alternative School*, it should be clear that I'm a firm believer in empowerment. I'm going to suggest, however, that many of the teacher-empowering strategies that are mentioned here can also apply to students. That's right—students! In successful alternative schools, everyone—teachers and students—should feel empowered.

Blase and Blase (1994) provide 13 suggestions for administrators who wish to initiate shared governance, a fundamental teacher-empowering experience:

1. Address your faculty and staff's readiness
2. Actively participate as an equal
3. Be enthusiastic
4. Ensure inclusion
5. Provide opportunities to meet
6. Be flexible
7. Support voluntary participation
8. Build trust
9. Protect the integrity of decisions and surrender power
10. Encourage a team spirit
11. Support risk
12. Encourage a problem-solving approach
13. Dare to challenge the status quo (pp. 51-56)

## Action Research as an Empowering Strategy

The use of "action research" can help empower teachers to work with at-risk students. Action research is different from the traditional kind of research that teachers engaged in during their college years. Instead of focusing upon theoretical problems, the action researcher attempts to solve real problems that confront her in the school or classroom. The solution (or intervention) should be data-driven, that is, based upon the teacher's careful analysis of the behaviors and performance—both written and nonwritten—of students in and out of the classroom. For example, teachers can chart or tally what students do in class, including behaviors such as volunteering to respond, participating in class discussions, and engaging in cooperative learning. Teachers should ask what students' written work might reveal about their cognitive and affective states. Questionnaires and interviews are also useful. Teachers can also perform research to determine how other professionals—faced with similar problems—responded.

Discussing action research, Gove and Kennedy-Calloway (1992) write,

> The teachers emphasized involvement and problem solving, themes related to ownership and its flip side, accountability. The systematic data collection led to focused, data-based feedback which gave the teachers impetus to change teaching routines that were often used, little thought out, and often ineffective. Analyzing the data collected in their classrooms in the action research process also reinforced their perception of task involvement, an important part of perceiving oneself as able to influence the learning of low-achieving children. . . . Research in teaching efficacy suggests that teachers are more likely to adopt new classroom strategies if they have confidence in their ability to control their classroom and affect student learning. . . . Thus, action research is an important staff development process. By engaging in it, teachers become empowered as they acquire and fine tune their teaching in specific and personal ways. (p. 533)

## Professionalism and Empowerment

Having administered alternative programs for many years, I'm used to the charges that alternative school teachers may not be acting in a "professional" manner in the methods that they use to award credit. Although I discussed the issue of credit awarding in other chapters, it bears repeating that any nontraditional credit-awarding model (i.e., proficiency or experiential based) will be criticized by a certain percentage of both educators and noneducators.

It's difficult for me to deal with these critics, especially when I see all the 17- and 18-year-old *freshman* who attend alternative schools. There is substantial research evidence that for the average student, retention in grade level does not improve achievement. Moreover, retention in grade level dramatically increases the likelihood that a student will quit school. Despite this research, retention is the number one strategy utilized by the great majority of schools in dealing with at-risk students. So for those who will question the professionalism of schools that award credits in nontraditional ways, I argue that parents should sue those traditional schools for malpractice when the schools retain at-risk students for 2, 3, sometimes even 4 years. Educators who retain students so frequently are not aware of what the literature in their profession indicates on the ineffectiveness of retention. To be unaware of the literature and appropriate practice in one's profession can be considered malpractice.

The point of my digression is that administration, faculty, and staff who work in alternative schools should become absolute professionals who are aware of the literature in their respective fields, who are committed to continual professional growth, and who *through their professionalism* are able to distance themselves from the day-to-day stresses that manage to burn out so many teachers in alternative schools.

What do I mean by, "are able to distance themselves...?" I certainly don't mean that teachers in alternative schools shouldn't care about their students. They should be able to distance themselves from depression and burn out, however—in much the same manner that physicians or nurses who work with seriously ill patients must distance themselves in order to continue to function successfully day after day—by developing a theoretical understanding of what is going on in their students' lives and the classroom. For example, what about students' use of obscenities? Many students in alternative programs frequently use what the general population would consider obscene language as a normal part of their linguistic patterns. At-risk students tend to use obscenities as adjectives and adverbs. Though their use of such language may upset some teachers, I tell my teachers that they have as much chance of jumping up and grabbing the moon out of the sky as they do in changing their students' speech patterns (or other indication of their culture) over a short period of time.

Language patterns can be altered over time. So, too, most of the problems of students in alternative programs can be successfully addressed over time. In programs that I've administered, it's taken about 18 school months for the typical at-risk student to overcome the cognitive and affective problems that have prevented her from achieving success. Just as it may take 7-10 days to cure a cold, I tell my teachers it's going to take 18 months to "cure" these adolescents. Teachers can choose to become upset or burned out because it takes about 18 months to accomplish this goal. Or, they can understand and conceptualize what is happening to students, and *as a professional* respond in the most appropriate manner and with the most effective strategies to their problems.

## Using Staff Development
## Sessions to Empower Teachers

Related to the concept of professionalism is staff development, which can help combat teacher burnout and stress by stimulating and renewing enthusiasm. Sessions should offer practical advice related to how to deal with ongoing problems faced in the classroom. In addition, the views of the staff should be incorporated in planning the staff development program, and the experience level of teachers should be considered in regard to staff development programs. Staff development should not be limited to one or two sessions each school year. Rather, it should provide continuous opportunities for professional and personal growth. These sessions can significantly change teachers' beliefs, knowledge, behavior, and the performance of their students. Teachers should be actively involved in the learning process, choosing goals and activities for themselves. If possible, the inclusion of personal professional goals should be integrated into staff development models, as well as visitations to other programs, retreats, workshops, and so forth. Training should be concrete, with an emphasis on demonstrations, supervised trials, and feedback.

Blase and Blase (1994) provide the following assumptions that underlie effective staff development efforts:

1. The principal is the guide or facilitator for staff development
2. Everyone can improve
3. Change comes from realizing that something is not quite right or not as good as it could be
4. Change is challenging and emotional
5. Teachers can teach each other
6. Staff development will take many forms
7. All educators engage in action research (pp. 61-62)

In addition, problem solving is critical to the process of organizational and staff development. Schmuck and Runkel (1985) believe problem solving to consist of the following elements:

1. Effective communication
2. Openness and trust

3. The ability to gather and use action research (consistently using available feedback and data related to effectiveness of programs to drive collective decision making and planning)

4. Conflict resolution (openly describing facts and feelings related to areas of dispute, searching for alternative solutions, committing to necessary changes, and action planning)

5. Effective group decision making (characterized by open communication, a sense of interpersonal trust, the fair chance of all to influence the decisions, and consensus—rather than majority, minority, or individual rule) (p. 113)

Although all teachers should experience the opportunity for empowerment, because of the difficult population that they work with teachers in alternative schools have a particularly pressing need to engage in reflective, participative, and improvement-oriented practice. A high level of commitment is necessary for faculty in alternative schools. They must be dedicated to the program, willing to risk and engage in experiential learning, and encouraged to participate in schoolwide decision making.

As we have already seen, the development of a culture of supportive interpersonal relationships is integral to the success of alternative programs. The administrator of the alternative school can facilitate the development of this culture by trusting teachers and encouraging innovation and autonomy, which are critical to shared governance and teacher empowerment.

# 9

# Involving Students
# in Their Own Education

Students who attend effective alternative schools are integrally involved in their own educational experience. When you visit one of these programs, you'll quickly sense that students feel in control of their learning and that they're excited about what goes on in the classroom. In this chapter, I'll discuss several principles or strategies that will help foster this high level of involvement.

Many of these suggestions involve a keen understanding of child and adolescent psychology. A teacher engages in hundreds of interactions with students each day. In traditional schools, interactions among at-risk students and their teachers and administrators are often unpleasant—sometimes even violent. Because so many of these exchanges are negative, students may wind up being assigned to or choosing to attend an alternative school. Even among highly skilled and experienced alternative teaching staff members, however, I have witnessed hundreds of minor interactions that—because a student was upset, angry, or disturbed in some other manner—escalated into significant confrontations. In order to avoid unpleasant confrontations and to lay the foundation for a culture that promotes student involvement, alternative school teachers should be aware of the importance of effective communication and relationship building. The following discussion focuses on relationships between children and their parents. Teachers should understand that the quality and nature of previous relationships with adult authority figures, particularly the child-parent relationship, integrally affects the expectations and attitudes that the student will bring with her or him to the classroom.

## The Difference Between Influence and Control

One of the most important points for promoting student involvement is to understand the distinction between influence and control. You should also understand that the parents and teachers of the great majority of students who eventually wind up attending an alternative school have—since the time they were small children—used control mechanisms to modify (or attempt to modify) their behavior. Thus, students who enter alternative schools are frequently coming from unpleasant family or school situations characterized by a control orientation. It is, in fact, *because* of their rebellion against such control mechanisms that many students are sent to or choose to attend an alternative program.

Gordon, clinical psychologist and founder of T.E.T. (Teacher Effectiveness Training) and P.E.T. (Parent Effectiveness Training), draws an important distinction between influence and control. Gordon (1991) writes,

> I firmly believe the single most important cause of the severe stress and strain in families during the adolescent years is that parents keep trying to use their power-based authority when in reality they no longer have any power. Then they ask, "What's gone wrong? Why doesn't discipline work anymore?" Most parents don't wake up to the fact that their powerlessness has left them without influence. The inevitable result of consistently employing power to control their kids when they are young is that parents never learn how to influence. When they reach adolescence, the kids can do whatever they wish—no controls, no restrictions. This is when parents are wrongly accused of being permissive. But they are not permissive parents; they are authoritarian parents who have lost their power. They are impotent parents who wish they weren't. (pp. 73-74)

I've heard a great many parents complain that their teenage daughter or son was well behaved as a child, but since she or he entered adolescence their behavior has deteriorated and the parents have lost control. I find it interesting that parents almost always use the phrase, "I've lost control." (It's also interesting that when traditional school administrators evaluate teachers, they place such a great emphasis on classroom "control.")

In more than 20 years of education, I've yet to hear a single parent say, "I've lost influence." Because it's so important, we need to examine more closely this process of "losing control."

There is a basic psychological paradox involving influence and control. You gain more influence with teenagers when you give up trying to control them. Conversely, the more that you attempt to control teenagers the less real influence you'll have over them. Look up the words *influence* and *control* in a thesaurus. You'll find that synonyms for *influence* include *teach, inform,* and *enlighten.* The process of influencing someone is intrinsically pleasant. On the other hand, when you *control* someone, you *restrict, punish,* and *regiment* her. The process of controlling someone is intrinsically unpleasant. Parents who complain that their teenager was once a pleasant, obedient child but has now turned into a disrespectful, unruly adolescent should recognize that their daughter or son may simply have outgrown the control mechanisms that previously proved effective in controlling her or him. The sad fact is that many parents may have never exercised influence over their children, even when they were very young. Parents were able to control children simply because they were small and weak. When children are young and helpless, parents are usually able to obtain control and compliance, regardless of their methods.

The most ineffective control mechanism is physical punishment. Many parents have told me of serious physical confrontations that occurred between them and their teenager. Several parents have remarked, "When my son was little, I'd just smack him and he'd obey. Now though, he's almost as big as me and he fights back. I don't know how to control him any longer." Some parents have told me they've had to call for police assistance to restrain their teenager during an altercation.

Clearly, getting tough (or tougher) is not the answer, and physical punishment should absolutely never be considered. I once saw a cartoon in *The New Yorker* magazine that illustrated the futility of the get tough approach. A parent is spanking his son, who is bottoms-up over his father's knee. The father says, "I hope this will teach you not to hit your baby brother."

Though we may laugh at this cartoon, most parents support corporal punishment in the schools. (Over the years I've had a great many parents tell me to strike their teen if she or he misbehaves in school.) At the same time, parents complain about the amount of violence in American society.

## Permissiveness Versus Authoritativeness: A False Choice

Many parents and teachers view the entire discipline issue as one of being either too permissive or too authoritative. Because no parent or teacher wants to be accused of being permissive, they tend to "get tough." Parents utilize control mechanisms—grounding, withdrawing privileges, depriving a teenager of a meal, sending him to his room—that can prove equally ineffective and frustrating as striking a child. The overwhelming majority of parents use some form of punishment as their primary means of control. Especially in teenagers, punishment usually only succeeds in fueling the fires of rebellion and revenge.

Similarly, traditional schools that follow "get tough" policies with disruptive or disaffected students experience little success. Gold and Mann (1982) write,

> There seems to be a growing consensus among educators, despite the lack of any reliable data, that the principal is a major determinant of the level of disruptiveness in a school. Furthermore, the consensus seems to be that firm discipline and organization are the hallmarks of effective principals. Our data on the importance of achieved flexibility suggest, on the other hand, that disruptive students may not respond so well to the projection of such a principal's style onto the school program if discipline and organization mean inflexibility. Certain students may be disruptive because they have chronic problems dealing with authority and because their frequent experiences of failure make any universal standards of behavior and performance threatening to them. If the principal is indeed a key element in minimizing school disruption, this study suggests that it is because his or her administration permits and encourages the staff to develop

more interpersonal relations even with the most disruptive students and to accommodate to their individuality. (p. 315)

Gordon (1991) points out,

The more I have learned about the principal causes of the behaviors that damage youth and weaken our society, the firmer my belief that our best hope for prevention is another kind of strategy—namely, helping adults who deal with children learn a new way to manage families, schools, and youth-oriented organizations. And that strategy will require teaching adults the skills required to govern their family, their classroom, their group more democratically, less autocratically—not the other way around as some are urging us to do. (p. xxix)

## The Importance of Effective Communication and Relationship Building

Effective communication is the best inoculation against difficult teenage behavior, including apathy. Communications issues underlie almost all interactions—including matters relating to discipline—between adults and teenagers. In fact, communication is so important that teachers and parents who can effectively communicate with teenagers will be faced with significantly fewer problems.

Teenagers and adults overwhelmingly indicate a desire to communicate with each other. Why then do so many teens and adults complain that they can't (or won't) talk to each other? The problem involves a lack of communication skills. Teachers who work in an alternative school must be exceptionally skilled communicators. They must be proactive—to become positively involved in adolescents' lives *before* serious problems arise—and to take the time to build a healthy relationship with their students.

Learning to communicate effectively with students is one of the most important skills in helping to build these positive relationships, which represent a kind of emotional bank account. By making frequent deposits in these emotional bank accounts, teachers can more effectively help teenagers through the inevitable troubles that will arise during adolescence. This "communication is critical mind-set" can permeate the entire school—from the involvement of students in discipline matters to the development of curriculum.

## Communication Blocks

When teenagers complain that their teachers don't listen to them, they really mean one of two things:

1. That teachers don't take the time to try to communicate with them
2. As is more often the case—that teachers take the time but lack effective communication skills

*All* teenagers—regardless of what they may say to the contrary—want to communicate with their teachers and parents. Teachers, however, often interrupt their teenager's attempt at real conversation with correcting messages such as lectures, accusations, and put downs. Also, with greater experience and wisdom, teachers are often tempted to take over the student's problem—and the conversation. Attempting to be "good teachers," they want to solve the student's problems, rather than allowing the teenager to try to figure things out for herself.

Teachers often inhibit communication by trying to talk teenagers out of their perceptions or feelings, explaining the "right" way to perceive or feel about a situation. They also inhibit real communication by allowing unresolved issues to get in the way, by interrupting to teach morality and value lessons, or by punishing. In fact, some teachers get so fixated on punishment that communication is virtually destroyed. There once was a cartoon that illustrated this point. Holding a stick, a father was chasing his son down the street. The boy's mother implored, "Please give him another chance." The father answered, "But he might not ever do it again!"

All these actions—especially punishment—represent forms of *communication blocks* that interrupt the listening process and prevent the development of real empathy and influence with the adolescence. Teachers should also be aware that when teenagers have something important they want to talk about, they sometimes bring up another issue first as a "test." This issue functions as a red herring or smoke screen. If teachers pass this initial test by not overreacting, becoming angry or overly upset, or blocking communication in some other way, then the student is likely to bring up the real issue.

## Other Communication-Impeding Mistakes

Ginott, a well-recognized authority on child rearing and author of *Between Parent & Teenager* (1969), has written about how important it is for adults to create *a healing dialogue* with adolescents and how communication blocks can prevent the creation of this dialogue. Ginott identifies seven common mistakes (he calls them "Seven Roads to Trouble") that adults make and that impede communication.

*1. Reasoning.* For the most part, adults are reasonable people (or at least we hope they behave in a reasonable manner). From the perspective and value systems of the teenager, most teenager behavior is entirely logical. Because the perspectives and value systems of adults and teenagers are different, however, teenagers don't generally behave in a manner that most adults would perceive as logical. Attempting to use adult reasoning on teenagers, then, can be as frustrating as trying to bail all the water out of the ocean with a paper cup.

*2. Clichés.* Teenagers can be reflective and introspective. They want real answers to their problems—not simplistic statements like "Rome wasn't built in a day," "You're very young, and your whole life is still in front of you," or "It's always darkest before the dawn." They resent adults who respond to their problems with trivialities or clichés.

*3. When I Was Your Age.* A sure turn-off, the "When I Was Your Age" lecture irritates teenagers. Many teenagers think that their teachers have been around since the time the earth was still cooling. The "When I Was Your Age" lecture also ignores the important fact that the world teenagers are growing up in is a much different place from the world in which their teachers grew up. Advice that may have been valid 20 years ago may no longer apply.

*4. Minimizing the Situation.* Certainly, in the course of an adolescent's entire life the end of a relationship or the loss of an after school job is not an earth-shattering event. Still, events such as these can *seem* traumatic to a teenager, who is likely to resent you for minimizing the extent of his hurt. Remember, though, that by adult standards, teenager behavior may not seem logical, and trying to persuade a teenager that she or he should feel different can prove counterproductive.

5. *The Trouble With You.* If you find yourself saying this—STOP! The basic rule of criticism is to avoid it if possible. Ginott (1969) writes that,

> Most criticism is unhelpful. It creates anger, resentment, and a desire for revenge. There are even worse effects. When a teenager is constantly criticized he learns to condemn himself and find fault with others. He learns to doubt his own worth, and to belittle the value of others. He learns to suspect people, and to expect personal doom. When we take a wrong turn on a road and lose our way, the last thing we need is criticism. (p. 77)

6. *Self-Pity.* Teenagers sometimes resent adults who pity them. Even more harmful, however, is the teacher whose attempts to be overly sympathetic may encourage the adolescent to wallow in self-pity.

7. *Pollyanna Approach.* This is really a spinoff of two different approaches (clichés and minimizing the situation). Everything does not always happen for the best. Also, teenagers resent it when teachers take a Pollyanna approach to their problems and say something like, "It's nothing to worry about. You'll have another boyfriend before the end of the week."

## Active Listening

If you rearrange the letters in the word LISTEN, you can form the word SILENT. Listening is the most important part of the communication process and its least developed skill. Learning when to remain silent is an important aspect of what's known as *Active Listening,* the all-purpose people skill. Active listening requires you to put aside whatever thoughts or feelings you have and listen carefully to teenagers. Through active listening, you help teenagers clarify feelings and alternatives, attempt to decode what they are really saying, and provide feedback (put their words into your own words and mirror it back) to let them realize that you understand the problem.

Try to remember what it was like when you were a teenager. How much did you really tell your parents? What were your worries and your dreams? How did you feel about your parents? How much privacy did you have? How did you feel when you lost a boyfriend or girlfriend? Active listening can help you develop a greater empathy with your teenager—to put yourself in her place. At the same time, however, don't emulate his language or conduct. Don't invite dependence either. Teachers should be empathetic adults—not teenage pals.

## Requirements for Active Listening

In order for active listening to work, teachers must be prepared to do the following:

1. Teachers must truly want to hear what a teenager has to say. And they must be willing to take as much time as necessary to listen. You can't appear preoccupied with something else when a student wants to talk to you.

2. They must be genuinely prepared to accept a student's feelings and what a teen has to say—no matter how much they may disagree with those feelings or dislike what a teen tells them. Questions such as, "What's wrong with you? Why can't you ... " can seriously damage the relationship. Also, because adolescence can be such a confusing time, a teen may genuinely not know what is wrong.

3. They must understand that feelings—like adolescence itself— can change quickly. Though they must respect teenagers' feelings and try to understand their point of view, they should also understand that those feelings are likely to change. Don't hold the fact that a teenager frequently changes his mind against him. That's part of growing into adulthood.

4. They must respect that a teenager is a separate human being, believe that she is capable of dealing with her own problems, and encourage the adolescent to try to find her own solutions to those problems. Accept her restlessness and discontent as real. Don't violate her privacy.

5. They must be open to having their view of the world challenged or changed by what a teenager says. Teachers should not hurry to correct facts. If they still disagree with what a

teenager says, it may be best to accept it but make sure the teen realizes that you don't approve of it.

## What About How Teachers Feel

The goal in practicing active listening is to establish effective, ongoing communication with teenagers. Part of this process involves *teachers communicating their thoughts and feelings* to teenagers. Not only do teachers have every right to explain how they feel, teenagers (contrary to what some difficult adolescents may say) really want to know how their teachers feel.

When teachers explain their thoughts and feelings, they should keep the following general principles in mind:

1. Don't be afraid to express your feelings.
2. Clearly state what you want. Make sure that you don't send contradictory messages.
3. Be brief and specific. Avoid clichés and preaching.
4. Be aware of your body language. Your body language should be consistent with the message that you're delivering. For example, if you're disciplining your teenager, don't smile. If you do, then you're sending the wrong message.
5. Use active listening and provide feedback.

## The Principle of Participation

Hundreds of studies have demonstrated that through the *principle of participation*, group members—including children and teenagers in families and schools—are more motivated to comply with mutually established rules; have greater levels of self-esteem, self-confidence, and-self discipline; and feel a greater sense of control over their fates. In addition, participative decision making can lead to more effective decisions as well as promote more positive relationships between teachers and students.

### Problem-Solving Process

*Prior to the development of a problem*, it's a good idea to establish a mutually agreed upon problem-solving process that can be used in the classroom when difficulties arise. The earlier you develop such a procedure with students, the better. Consider this a preventive measure. A typical problem-solving process might include the following phases:

1. Problem Definition
2. Identification of Possible Solutions
3. Discussion of the Pros and Cons of Each Possible Solution
4. Choosing the Best Solutions
5. Development of a Plan to Implement the Solution
6. Follow-up and Revision

Whether you actually identify all possible solutions and choose the best plan and method to implement the plan is not that important. The important point is that you're engaging in a *process* that can significantly improve communication between you and your students. Manage your classroom with a power-with philosophy, as opposed to a power-over philosophy. On a schoolwide basis, peer mediation programs accomplish a similar objective.

## New Paradigms for Managing Schools and Classrooms

I could list many more suggestions to involve students integrally in their own education. All of these suggestions, however, revolve around certain common themes, such as communication, relationship building, and democratic school governance. And taken together, these common themes create a new paradigm for managing schools and classrooms.

Gibbons (1984) writes,

Our new paradigm must promise to produce better education with fewer resources and to restore our profession to a place of pride in the community; it must make public education a highly desirable alternative that meets the challenge of a new technology, enables students to deal with a rapidly changing society and workplace, and prepares them to deal with the incredible national and global problems we now face. In addition, our paradigm must teach higher-order skills through high-impact teaching methods, develop the talents of all individuals as fully as possible, cultivate social skills and responsibilities, encourage students to develop their inner drives and express them through their learning activities, and insure that students are well-equipped for a lifetime of learning. Challenging tasks all, they are the real challenges we face. (p. 91)

Psychologists Corsini and Lombardi (1988) developed a new model for schooling that is known as the Corsini Four-R system (C4R). They write,

C4R is a learning environment based on mutual respect in which children are treated as equals with adults (parents and faculty), with rights and obligations established by a "constitution" which governs the school's functioning based essentially on the American ideal of democracy. The C4R system advances four goals for student development: *responsibility* (to be built by involving children in decisions about their own education, under close realistic guidelines), *respect* (to be nurtured by treating students with respect and by requiring respect), *resourcefulness* (encouraged by opportunities to prepare for three main life tasks: occupation and leisure, family life, and membership in society), and *responsiveness* (encouraged by striving for a school environment in which people demonstrate trust in others and caring for others). (cited in Gordon, 1991, pp. 144-145)

In writing about the C4R method, Gordon (1991), founder of the Parent Effectiveness Training (P.E.T) program and the Teacher Effectiveness Training (T.E.T) program, states that,

Here are some of the more unusual aspects of C4R: (1) Children have considerable options on where to be and what to do during the school day; (2) children have five different modes for learning academic subjects: (a) in class, (b) studying in the library, (c) studying with peers, (d) working with teacher/advisor, (e) studying in their home; (3) every child has a self-selected faculty member as his/her teacher/advisor; (4) there are no grades; (5) the kind and degree of learning is based on objectives tests given weekly in terms of specific units of instruction; (6) faculty are not to communicate with parents unless the child is present; (7) children "nominate" faculty members as advisors, but once a faculty member accepts a child as a counselee, only the child can make changes to another teacher/advisor; (8) there are no report cards, only weekly progress reports to *students* who are advised to show them to their parents; (9) children set their own pace of learning and can be simultaneously studying subjects at different levels; (10) no rewards, honors, or special attention given to children for academic performance. . . . The C4R rules are the following: (1) Do nothing that could be dangerous or damaging; (2) Always be in a supervised place or en route from one supervised place to another; (3) If a teacher signals you to leave a classroom, do so immediately and in silence. (p. 145)

## Final Comments on Involving
## Students in Their Own Education

Don't become discouraged if students seem resistant at first to assuming a greater role in their own education. Remember that in their traditional schools most at-risk students were perceived as "undesirables," and teachers frequently attempted to appease them— "Don't bother me and I'll give you a C"—with low-level academic work. Teachers certainly didn't ask disruptive students to participate in the governance of the classroom. Just as at-risk students may initially believe that busy work is "real work" and that assignments involving higher-order thinking skills are "weird," so too they may perceive your attempts to involve them in their own education as strange. Once this initial resistance is overcome, however, you will be amazed how students who had been perceived as undesirables in one location can flourish and become self-directed learners in your alternative school.

# 10

# Evaluating Alternative Programs

I saved the chapter on evaluating alternative programs until last because there are serious questions involving the efficacy of many of the evaluations that have been conducted of alternative schools. Related to these problems is the fact that a decided "anti-evaluation" sentiment exists among many proponents of alternative education. This anti-evaluation sentiment seems to originate from two general sources:

1. a kind of "antiestablishment" attitude that is prevalent among some members of the alternative education community
2. the severe nature of the problems that afflict a sizable percentage of students who attend alternative programs and the close bond that tends to form between alternative school faculty and students

Many teachers in the alternative education community seem to believe that because they are so dedicated to rescuing students from the most serious of social pathologies—including suicidal ideation, substance abuse, runaway behavior, acts of juvenile delinquency and gang involvement, and parental abuse—they should not be held accountable (or be held less accountable than teachers in traditional schools) for student achievement. Although I would consider myself a member of the alternative education community, I reject this line

123

of reasoning. Yes, of course it's more important to prevent an at-risk adolescent from attempting suicide or abusing drugs than it is to improve her reading or writing skills. Yes, of course it's more important to prevent an at-risk adolescent from engaging in acts of promiscuity or juvenile delinquency than it is to improve her math skills. Still, *rescuing an at-risk teenager from social pathologies is not enough.* I've always told my teachers that teaching in an alternative school may be the most difficult assignment that they will ever face. Together, alternative school teachers and administrators must take responsibility for both the affective and cognitive development of their students.

Having spent many years as a principal of several alternative programs, I'm aware of the close bonds that form between teachers and students and the genuine desire that teachers experience to help students achieve success. Though these close relationships are an integral part of the success of alternative schools, at the same time because of these close relationships teachers may feel pressured to award credits for academic work that is not comparable to work completed in a traditional school. Because teachers in alternative programs empathize with the struggles that their students are experiencing, they may want them to succeed (i.e., earn a high school diploma), regardless of their level of academic competence.

This phenomenon occurs in all schools; however, the effect is far more concentrated in alternative schools, given the nature of the students who attend these programs.

## Problems With Early Evaluations

The anti-evaluation sentiment I mentioned earlier, though still prevalent, was much stronger in the 1960s and 1970s. Duke and Muzio reviewed evaluations conducted in the 1970s of 19 alternative schools. They listed the most serious problems with these evaluations as:

Lack of control or comparison group
Poor record keeping
No randomized sample of students, teachers, and parents
Failure to report data on program dropouts
Lack of pre-posttest comparison

Lack of follow-up on dropouts and early graduates of programs. (Duke & Muzio study cited in Young, 1990, p. 37)

As alternative programs proliferated throughout the 1970s and 1980s, more rigorous evaluations were conducted. In the next section, I'll review a few of the better known of these evaluations.

## Sample of Alternative Education Evaluations

Foley (1983) reported on a study of 10 alternative public high schools in New York City. The author writes,

A preliminary assessment compared credit accumulation and attendance data for the fall of 1981 for 25 percent of incoming students at eight alternative schools with similar data from their earlier high school careers. On average, this group of nearly 300 students earned 60 percent more credits and cut their absences by nearly 40 percent—clearly an important break from past practices. . . . Repeatedly, students expressed real satisfaction about their relationships with teachers; about the safe, nonviolent and caring atmosphere of their schools; and about the educational programs that they perceived as well suited to their needs and interests. . . . When data from students and faculty interviews were taken together, we began to glimpse what dropout and truant youngsters require of their schools: structure and support, close interpersonal relationships, flexibility, a curriculum that helps them understand the world and their own lives, and continuity toward a diploma. (p. 59)

Smith, Gregory, and Pugh (1981) developed an instrument called Statements About Schools (SAS) that is based upon Abraham Maslow's hierarchy of needs. The instrument was designed to assess how well a school satisfies the needs of its students, as determined by the reports of both students and teachers. The authors used the Statements About Schools Instrument to assess students in seven alternative and six comprehensive high schools located in four states.

Smith et al. (1981) reported that,

Students in the alternative schools were much more satisfied with how well their schools were meeting their needs than were students in the conventional schools. The differences in comparable schools for teachers . . . are very large. The teachers in the lowest-scoring alternative school are far more satisfied with their success in meeting students' needs, especially in the top three scales in the hierarchy, than are their counterparts in the highest-scoring conventional school. . . . We cannot identify a cause for such differences since our study was not designed to establish causality. There is, however, only one variable that all the alternatives have in common: free choice. Teachers and students have freely chosen to work and study in these schools. The "ownership" of and identification with these schools that seem to result from the simple act of choosing is the variable to which we are most inclined to attribute the large differences we found, but this conclusion must remain speculative for now. (p. 562)

Blank (1994) studied 15 school districts and 45 magnet schools in urban school settings. The author reported that,

The schools in our study produced consistently higher attendance rates, fewer behavioral problems, and lower suspension and dropout rates. . . . Those magnet schools that offered high-quality education generally benefitted from extensive community involvement and support. Businesses and industries, institutions of higher education, community organizations, and parents all contributed to the special programs that these schools offered. The contributions varied from one district to another, but they often included assisting with program design or curriculum development, providing part-time instructors, or loaning facilities and equipment to the school. (p. 270)

Raywid (1984) surveyed 2,500 alternative programs. Twelve hundred schools responded to the author's study, which was primarily descriptive in nature. Raywid reported that the following qualities characterized these 1,200 alternative programs:

High staff morale; 90% of teachers felt strong ownership of their programs.

Increased student attendance; 81% of schools reported student attendance had increased or greatly increased compared to patterns at previous schools.

Good student-teacher relationships; 63% of the schools identified student-teacher interaction as their most distinctive feature.

Smallness; 69% of the students had fewer than 200 students.

Choice; 79% of the students were there by choice. (p. 70)

Young (1990) writes,

Academic achievement as well as the attitudes of delinquent students attending alternative and conventional schools were analyzed by Martin Gold and David Mann (1982) in *Expelled to a Friendlier Place*. The authors compared approximately sixty at-risk students from three alternative secondary schools with a matched group of students from conventional secondary schools in the same districts. Alternative and conventional students were matched by age, sex, grade point average, discipline history, self-esteem, and attitude toward school. Pre- and posttest results over the school year were the basis for comparison. The authors concluded that, "Alternative students were significantly less disruptive in school at the end of the study than conventional students. Teachers rated alternative students better behaved than conventional students. Alternative students were significantly more positive about school and confident in their role as students than conventional students. While alternative students received slightly improved grades when they reenrolled in conventional schools, their achievement test scores did not improve and were not different from those of conventional students." (p. 41)

## Philosophical Issues Related to the Evaluation of Alternative Schools

What can we make of these evaluations? Are there different parameters that should be applied to evaluations of alternative programs as compared with traditional programs?

Although more rigorous evaluations of alternative programs are now taking place, the research base for these programs is still extremely limited. From the evaluations discussed in the preceding paragraphs (as well as other evaluations of alternative programs), it is clear that alternative schools can be extremely effective in meeting the affective needs of students. In addition, students attending alternative schools generally demonstrate improved attendance and earn more credits when compared with their performance in a traditional school.

What is not so clear, however, is the effect that alternative programs have on student achievement. Depending upon the population defined as "alternative" (and remember that magnet schools serving intellectually gifted students are considered alternative programs by many researchers), as well as the research design and methodologies used in studying achievement in alternative schools, the results as to the effect of alternative schools on academic achievement are often confusing and contradictory.

Should alternative schools be evaluated according to different principles or standards? Because so many students would quit or be removed from school entirely if they had not been placed in an alternative school, should evaluators of alternative schools conduct an "alternative" evaluation?

I believe that evaluators of alternative programs should conduct the most broad-based evaluation possible, including an analysis of all pertinent affective and cognitive data that are available. This is not to argue that academic achievement is not of importance in determining the success of a program. Academic achievement, however, should be considered one component of a comprehensive program evaluation.

Before we look at a comprehensive model for evaluating an alternative school, two other important issues should be discussed.

## *If We Can Save Just One*

I've heard hundreds of administrators and teachers in alternative schools say that, "If we can save just one child from a life of unemployment, underemployment, or criminal behavior, then this program is worth every dollar that it costs to maintain it." You should recognize that this argument, though reflecting laudable compassion for troubled children and adolescents, becomes specious when applied to the issue of program evaluation. Because there is only a finite amount of money and other resources in the world, unless an alternative school—or any other school or social program, for that matter—can demonstrate cost-effectiveness when compared to other comparable programs or intervention efforts, then that school should not receive financial and other scare resources to ensure its continued operation. Cost-effectiveness relates to the efficacy of a program in achieving given intervention outcomes in relation to program costs. If a program is not cost-effective, financial and other forms of support should be redirected to programs with a proven record of success, with success having been determined by a comprehensive program evaluation.

## *Effect of More Rigorous Graduation Standards*

Across the United States, many states have begun to institute more rigorous graduation standards, including passing state-mandated examinations in subjects like reading, writing, and mathematics. I have ambivalent feelings about the effect of more rigorous graduation standards on at-risk students. The better alternative programs should have no problem in achieving both cognitive and affective objectives, and most students in these quality programs should successfully meet the more rigorous academic standards. You may recall from earlier chapters, however, that I argue that the substantial majority of programs that are called "alternative" are alternative in name only and that these programs produce few significant cognitive or affective changes in students. Consequently, a large number of ineffective "alternative" programs will either have to undergo a profound transformation and become truly effective alternative schools, or they will be closed because of students' inability to meet the more rigorous academic standards. And that brings us to the question: Is any alternative program—effective or ineffective—better than no alternative program at all? It will require a comprehensive program evaluation to answer this question.

## Comprehensive Program Evaluation

Any evaluation of an alternative program must be as comprehensive as possible. This evaluation should consider traditional data such as academic achievement, number of credits earned, attendance, discipline referrals, days lost to suspension, and so forth. The evaluation should also include important affective and health-related data, such as information concerning substance use and abuse; incidents of depression, mental illness, and suicide attempts; involvement in acts of delinquent behavior; the number of students who have babies; and changes in the quality of students' relationships with significant adults.

The use of affective and health-related data is extremely important. Consider the following . . . the United States currently spends more than $500 billion on social welfare programs. In some states, more than 80% of the prison population are school dropouts. Of minority dropouts, 65% are unemployed. Only 27% of male dropouts and 31% of female dropouts even try to look for work. The great majority of burglaries and break-ins are committed by jobless teenagers. Each year, 600,000 girls have to leave school to have babies. More than 80% of these girls will never return to school. America's economic health is threatened by the nation's high dropout rate. A permanent and enlarging underclass is developing.

Because many potential members of this permanent underclass wind up attending alternative schools, it is imperative that any evaluation of an alternative program consider nonacademic data as well as traditional academic information. An alternative school may not do a very good job in improving test scores; however, if the program succeeds in reducing acts of social pathologies or instilling a successful work ethic in students, a legitimate argument can be made that the program—viewed strictly from cost-benefit perspective—could be considered successful in terms of overall long-term benefits produced for society.

To conduct such a comprehensive evaluation of an alternative program requires more skills than most local program evaluators will possess. Not only does the evaluator have to obtain comprehensive affective and cognitive data (some of which may not be available in the school or which may be sensitive information that the students' families might wish to conceal), the evaluator will also have to attach cost estimates to these data, as well as consider several other difficult matters in reaching conclusions concerning program effectiveness.

One of the leading authorities on evaluation, Scriven (1981) writes that,

Evaluation is an extremely complicated discipline, what one might call a multi-discipline. It cannot be seen as straightforward application of standard methods in the traditional social science repertoire. In fact, only seven of the fifteen checkpoints are seriously addressed in the traditional repertoire, and in most cases not very well addressed as far as evaluation needs are concerned. (p. 83)

The "checkpoints" that Scriven refers to are 15 points of a Key Evaluation Checklist (KEC) that he has used in conducting comprehensive program evaluations. A brief item-by-item KEC summary follows.

1. *Description:* What is to be evaluated? Does it have components? The description may be divided into four parts: nature and operation; the function; the delivery system; the support system.

2. *Client:* Who is commissioning the evaluation?

3. *Background & Context:* Includes identification of stakeholders; function and nature of the program; believed performance; expectations from the evaluation; desired type of evaluation; reporting system; organization charts; history of project; and prior evaluation efforts.

4. *Resources:* Sometimes called the "strengths assessment" by contrast with the needs assessment of Checkpoint 6. They are not what *is* used up, in for example, purchase or maintenance, but what *could* be. They include money, expertise, past experience, technology, and flexibility considerations.

5. *Consumer:* Who is using or receiving the effects of the program?

6. *Values:* Sometimes called the "needs assessment" of the impacted and potentially impacted populations; the defined goals of the program when a goal-based evaluation is undertaken.

7. *Process:* What constraints and values apply to, and what conclusions can we draw about the normal *operation* of the program (as opposed to its effects or outcomes)? In particular, legal/ethical/political/managerial/aesthetic/hedonic/ scientific constraints. With this checkpoint we begin to draw evaluative conclusions.

8. *Outcomes:* What effects (long-term outcomes or concurrent effects) are produced by the program (intended or unintended)? A matrix of effects is useful to get one started on the search: population affected × type of effect (cognitive/affective/ psychomotor/health/social/environmental) × size of each × time of onset (immediate/end of "treatment"/later) × duration × each component.

9. *Generalizability:* To other people, places, times, and versions.

10. *Costs:* Including dollar, psychological, personnel, time, initial, recurrent, direct, indirect, immediate, delayed, and discounted.

11. *Comparisons:* With alternative options—recognized and unrecognized.

12. *Significance:* A synthesis of all the above.

13. *Recommendations:* May or may not be requested.

14. *Report:* Includes length, format, medium, and so forth.

15. *Meta-evaluation:* An evaluation of the evaluation before dissemination.

A discussion of the Key Evaluation Checklist and how to utilize the KEC in conducting program evaluations could compose the entire curriculum in a graduate course on evaluation. Readers interested in learning how to conduct such a comprehensive evaluation should consult Scriven's *Evaluation Thesaurus* (1981). Three other works that I recommend are James Sanders's (1992) *Evaluating School Programs: An Educator's Guide*, Rita O'Sullivan and Cheryl Tennant's (1992) *Programs for At-Risk Students: A Guide to Evaluation*, and Joan Herman and Lynn Winters's *Tracking Your School's Success* (1992). All three books are published by Corwin Press.

If you're interested in conducting such a comprehensive program evaluation, I suggest that unless you have substantial experience in this kind of broad-based evaluative effort, you consider hiring an outside evaluator. If financial restraints preclude you from hiring an outside evaluator and you must conduct your own evaluation of the alternative school, remember that it is of critical importance to analyze as much data as possible related to affective, social, health issues, and so forth. Also, you'll need to establish parameters as to how much these measures should "count" in your conclusions and recommendation, as compared with traditional pre/post measures such as achievement on standardized tests, credits earned, and attendance.

## A Final Comment Concerning
## Evaluations of Alternative Schools

I believe that any program or school should be evaluated in as comprehensive a manner as possible, given whatever limits are imposed by time, finances, expertise, and the availability of other resources. This kind of broad-based evaluative approach becomes even more important when evaluating alternative schools. Academic achievement, credits earned, and attendance cannot be the only data analyzed in order to obtain a fair and accurate understanding of the alternative program. On the other hand, academic achievement is extremely important, and alternative schools must not forsake this responsibility by concentrating *an inordinate amount of time and energy* in attempting to rescue at-risk students from social pathologies. Effective alternative schools help students meet all their needs and goals.

# Conclusion

I reread *How to Establish an Alternative School* over a weekend. The manuscript was complete; however, I needed a conclusion. I didn't want the conclusion to include any more theory or research. There's enough theory and research in the manuscript as it is. I wanted the conclusion to come from my heart—rather than my mind. I wanted the reader to understand what it *feels* like to run a successful alternative school.

I decided to wait until the end of a particularly difficult day at the alternative school to write my conclusion. Though there are no easy days at alternative schools, today was unusually rough. There are some days when everything seems to happen all at once—like a whole freight train full of troubles rushing down upon you. Then there are days when the problems come one after another—like an endless chain of falling dominoes. Today, it felt like both those kinds of days!

Around 11 a.m., I felt the pressure starting to squeeze me like a vice. It wouldn't let up for the rest of the day.

Right now, it's 5 p.m. and the phone is still ringing. I still have several calls to make to parents, other school administrators, probation officers, the police, substance abuse counselors, and so forth. There's plenty of paperwork that has to be completed, too.

I'm supposed to be an expert on alternative education. Sometimes I wonder what that really means—especially at the end of difficult days like this one. As I reflect on the day, however, I realize that the kids, faculty, staff, and I made it through another day, nobody got into any really serious trouble, there were no fights, nobody got suspended or arrested, no incidents of substance abuse or vandalism. And in the process, some adolescents who can be very difficult benefited from another day of education and counseling.

I imagine I dealt with at least one hundred difficult situations today. Holding the stress in check, I managed never to lose my temper or become angry. I used as much theory and psychology as I know—and as many other skills as I possess—to help these kids make it through another day. And I'm prepared to come back tomorrow, when I know I'll face the same set of problems. More than anything else, that's what it takes to administer a successful alternative school.

You probably read *How to Establish an Alternative School* in the comfort and quiet of your home or office. I suggest that you reread this book, studying it as if it were a textbook. When it comes time for you to apply the advice in *How to Establish an Alternative School*, you won't have the luxury of comfort or quiet. You'll be on the firing line . . . that's when the fun starts.

Don't allow the pressure of working with at-risk youth to shake your professionalism or commitment. No matter how difficult their behavior may be, don't become upset or angry. Hold students accountable for their behavior, but don't become punitive. Always go back to the theory . . . do what the literature suggests is correct . . . be a professional.

It's simple to chase kids down a hallway with a baseball bat or throw them out of school. It's a lot harder to help them redirect their lives in a positive manner. But that's what those who work in successful alternative schools do.

It's not easy. It never will be.

As I think back . . . maybe today wasn't so bad after all.

Good luck with your alternative school.

# Resource A

## References

Bierlein, J., & Vandergrift, J. (1993). Educating the at-risk in Arizona: Lessons from the past and directions for the future. *ASBA Journal, 23*(4), 4-6.

Blank, R. (1984). The effects of magnet schools on the quality of education in urban school districts. *Phi Delta Kappan, 66*(4), 270-272.

Blase, J., & Blase, J. R. (1994). *Empowering teachers: What successful principals do.* Newbury Park, CA: Corwin.

Bloom, B. (1956). *Taxonomy of educational objectives: The classification of educational goals: Handbook 1. Cognitive domain.* New York: David McKay.

Bodinger-DeUriarte, C., & Sancho, A. (1992). *Hate crimes: Sourcebook for schools.* Los Alamitos, CA: Southwest Regional Laboratory, and Philadelphia: Research for Better Schools.

Catello, J., & Peck, K. (1990). Instructional alternatives for at-risk students. *Media & Methods, 26*(5), 12, 54-57.

Coleman, J. S., Campbell, E. Q., Hobson, C., McPartland, J.A.M., Weinfeld, F. D., & York, R. L. (1966). *Equality of educational opportunity.* Washington, DC: Government Printing Office.

Comer, J. (1987, March). New Haven's school-community connection. *Educational Leadership,* pp. 13-16.

Dawson, J. (1987, October). Helping at-risk students in middle schools. *NASSP Bulletin,* pp. 84-88.

Doyle, D., & Levine, M. (1984). Magnet schools: Choice and quality in public education. *Phi Delta Kappan, 66*(4), 265-270.

Edwards, C. (1989). Self-regulation: The key to motivating at-risk children. *The Clearing House, 63*(2), 58-62.

Ficklen, E. (1990). Detours on the road to drugs. *American School Board Journal, 177*(2), 19-22.

Fingerhut, L., & Kleinman, J. (1990). International and interstate comparisons of homicide among male youth. *Journal of the American Medical Association, 263*(24), 3292.

Fizzell, R. (1985, September). *Alternative education.* Paper presented at the conference, "Building Alliances Toward Better and Safer Schools," Chicago.

Foley, E. (1983). Alternative schools: New findings. *Social Policy, 13*(3), 44-46.

Gibbons, M. (1984). Walkabout ten years later: Searching for renewed vision of education. *Phi Delta Kappan, 65*(9), 591-600.

Ginott, H. (1969). *Between parent & teenager.* New York: Avon Books.

Gold, M., & Mann, D. (1982). Alternative schools for troublesome secondary students. *Urban Review, 14*(4), 305-316.

Gordon, T. (1991). *Discipline that works: Promoting self-discipline in children.* New York: Penguin.

Gove, M., & Kennedy-Calloway, C. (1992). Action research: Empowering teachers to work with at-risk students. *Journal of Reading, 35*(7), 526-534.

Gregory, T. (1988, Summer). What makes alternative schools alternative? *Holistic Education Review,* p. 12.

Hahn, A. (1987). Reaching out to America's drop outs: What to do? *Phi Delta Kappan, 69*(4), 256-263.

Hancock, V. (1993). The at-risk student. *Educational Leadership, 50*(4), 84-85.

Herman, J., & Winters, L. (1992). *Tracking your school's success.* Newbury Park, CA: Corwin.

Hudelson, D. (1994). School-to-work transition. *Vocational Education Journal, 69*(3), 17.

Hunter, R., & Kellam, S. (1990). Prevention begins in the first grade. *Principal, 50*(2), 17-19.

Jennings, W., & Nathan, J. (1977). Startling/disturbing research on school program effectiveness. *Phi Delta Kappan, 65*(9), 568-572.

Kalish, C. (1988). *International crime rates. Bureau of Justice special report.* Washington, DC: U.S. Department of Justice.

Knapp, M., Shields, P., & Turnbull, B. (1990). New directions for educating the children of poverty. *Educational Leadership, 48*(1), 4-8.

Lieberman, J. (1985). *A practical partnership.* New York: LaGuardia Community College. (ERIC Document Reproduction Service No. ED 258 640)

Melenyzer, B. J. (1993). *Teacher empowerment: The discourse, meanings, and social actions of teachers.* Paper presented at the annual conference of the National Council on Inservice Education, Orlando, FL.

Miller, R. (1994). *What are schools for: Holistic education in American culture.* Brandon, VT: Holistic Education Press.

Mintz, J. (Ed.). (1994). *The handbook of alternative education.* New York: Macmillan.

National Association for Mediation in Education. (1990). *Rationale for starting a program packet.* Amherst, MA: Author.

Olinger, D. (1991, October 6). Kids and guns. *St. Petersburg Times,* p. 1D.

O'Sullivan, R., & Tennant, C. (1992). *Programs for at-risk students.* Newbury Park, CA: Corwin.

Raywid, M. (1984). Synthesis of research on schools of choice. *Educational Leadership, 41*(7), 70-78.

Raywid, M. (1988). Why are alternatives successful? *Holistic Education Review, 1*(2), 27-28.

Raywid, M. (1990). Alternative education: The definition problem. *Changing Schools, 18,* 4-5, 10.

Sanders, J. (1992). *Evaluating school programs: An educator's guide.* Newbury Park, CA: Corwin.

Schlemmer, P. (1981). The zoo school: Evolution of an alternative. *Phi Delta Kappan, 62*(8), 558-560.

Schmuck, R., & Runkel, P. (1985). *The handbook of organizational development in schools.* Palo Alto, CA: Mayfield.

Scriven, M. (1981). *Evaluation thesaurus.* Inverness, CA: Edge Press.

Senge, P. (1990). *The fifth discipline: The art & practice of the learning organization.* Garden City, NY: Doubleday.

Smith, G. R., Gregory, T. B., & Pugh, R. C. (1981). Meeting student needs: Evidence for the superiority of alternative schools. *Phi Delta Kappan, 62*(8), 561-564.

St. Pierre, R., & Miller, D. (1986, January). Future directions for school-based alcohol education. *Health Education,* pp. 11-13.

Sweeney, M. (1988). Alternative education and alternative schools. *Holistic Education Review, 1*(2), 22-25.

Sweeney, M., & Wheelock, A. (1989). Alternative education: A vehicle for school reform. *Changing Schools, 17*(3), 1, 4-6.

Van Ruiten, J. (1990). Catching them early. *Thrust for Educational Leadership, 20*(2), 19-22.

Wachtel, T., York, D., & York, P. (1983). *Toughlove.* New York: Bantam.

Wagner, J. (1989). *Ethnographic work and educational administration: Reframing problematics of educational research and practice.* Davis: University of California, Division of Education. (ERIC Document Reproduction Service No. ED 312 273)

Wircenski, J., & Others. (1990). Instructional alternatives. *NASSP Curriculum Report, 19*(4), 2-7.

Wright, J. D., Rossi, P. H., Daly, K., & Weber-Burdin, E. (1983). *Under the gun: Weapons, crime and violence in America.* New York: Aldine.

Young, T. (1990). *Public alternative education: Options and choice for today's schools.* New York: Teachers College Press.

# Resource B

## Sources for More Information

One of the reasons I wrote *How to Establish an Alternative School* was to provide a comprehensive reference for readers who are interested in starting their own programs. There are very few publications that deal directly with this topic.

There are, however, two books that I would highly recommend as sources for more information on establishing an alternative school. These are *The Handbook of Alternative Education*, edited by Jerry Mintz and Raymond and Sidney Solomon and published by Macmillan, and the Phi Delta Kappan Center for Evaluation, Development, and Research publication, *The Alternative School Choice*.

### The Handbook of Alternative Education

The title, *The Handbook of Alternative Education*, strikes me as a bit misleading in that Mintz and his coeditors have written what is primarily a directory of alternative education programs throughout the United States. Though the work includes several interesting essays on alternative schools, the real value of *The Handbook of Alternative Education* is the detailed state-by-state listing of programs, complete with contact persons and phone numbers. If you're interested in talking with people involved in the alternative education movement or visiting alternative schools, this is an excellent reference book.

## *The Alternative School Choice*

*The Alternative School Choice* provides 32 essays about alternative education selected from various journals, books, and conferences. Read from cover to cover, *The Alternative School Choice* offers a summary of the most important research on alternative education and is an excellent reference for anyone who plans to establish an alternative school.

## Other Sources

A few other works or sources that may be useful as you proceed with plans to establish your own program are listed below.

Glasser, W. (1990). *The quality school: Managing students without coercion.* New York: Harper & Row.

Herman, J., & Winters, L. (1992). *Tracking your school's success.* Newbury Park, CA: Corwin.

Mintz, J. *The newsletter of the Alternative Education Resource Organization.* Roslyn, NY.

O'Sullivan, R., & Tennant, C. (1992). *Programs for at-risk students.* Newbury Park, CA: Corwin.

Sanders, J. (1992). *Evaluating school programs: An educator's guide.* Newbury Park, CA: Corwin.

Sizer, T. R. (1984). *Horace's compromise: The dilemma of the American high school.* Boston: Houghton Mifflin.

Many states have associations of alternative educators. Contact your state department of education for additional information and to find out how to get in touch with your state association. Also, your state department of education can provide you with any special guidelines or regulations that may apply as you establish your own alternative school.

Finally, I invite readers to contact me if you feel I can be of additional assistance:

John Kellmayer, Ed.D.
P.O. Box 47
Haddonfield, NJ 08033

# Index